Additional Praise for *Family Trusts*

"In Chap. 1 of *Loring and Rounds: A Trustee's Handbook,* the authors remind its readers that the Anglo-American trust is an ancient principles-based regime that will survive into the 21st century only so long as it is administered by persons of principle. As a practical matter, what does that mean? *Family Trusts* does an admirable job of answering that question, and in prose that will be readily understandable not only to the trust professional but also to the family member new to the 'trustscape.' "

**—Charles E. Rounds, Jr., Professor of Law,
Suffolk University Law School**

"At long last—a clear and concise guidebook for those who don't understand the complexities of family trusts! The three authors offer practical strategies and sample documents for many trust challenges—why to set up a trust, how to select a good trustee, and how to be a good trustee or beneficiary. Start with the chapter that applies to your case, and you will be compelled to read the other related chapters. And grantors need to read it all, before they sign or revise their estate plans."

**—Sara Hamilton, Founder and CEO,
Family Office Exchange**

"A trust is a powerful tool that too often turns beneficiaries into trust-fund babies, creates resentments and rifts among family members, and ultimately deforms many a family's legacy. *Family Trusts* helps wealthy families and their advisors avoid those outcomes by building what they call a 'comprehensive model for a humane trustscape.' No grantor should plan their estate, no beneficiary should accept their next check, and no advisor should meet with their next client without first reading this book."

—Angelo Robles, Founder & Chairman,
Family Office Association

"The authors tell us that 80% of beneficiaries view trusts as a burden, yet over 90% of private wealth is tied-up in some form of trust by the time of the third generation. Hence these trusts become 'arranged marriages' between the beneficiaries and the trustees. This insightful guide walks one through how to best prepare for that 'meteor moment' by focusing on the creating the best culture for these new arrangements to not only survive, but flourish."

—Thomas R. Livergood, Founder & CEO,
The Family Wealth Alliance

"Jay has outdone himself once again! *Family Trusts* combines his and his co-authors' many years of trust wisdom with a practical and theoretical guide to both creating and administering trusts with an important emphasis on family values. Hartley, Jay, and Keith's eminent qualifications to author such a book are powerfully displayed throughout. The book is a must read for all trust professionals!"

—Al King III, Co-CEO, South Dakota
Trust Company LLC

Family Trusts

Family Trusts

A Guide for Beneficiaries, Trustees, Trust Protectors, and Trust Creators

HARTLEY GOLDSTONE

JAMES E. HUGHES JR.

KEITH WHITAKER

ISBN 9781119118268 (Hardcover)
ISBN 9781119118299 (ePDF)
ISBN 9781119118282 (ePub)

Printed in the United States of America

SKY10080508_072524

Dedication

To Loyce, Ben, and Jon
— Hartley Goldstone

*To Patricia M. Angus, Richard Bakal, and Joanie Bronfman,
my fellow journeyers for nearly 30 years on the path to change
beneficiaries' views of their trusts from burdens to blessings, and
to Jacqueline Merrill, who put her arm through mine.*
— James E. Hughes Jr., Esq.

*To my mother, who trusted me,
and to my father, who taught me to be trustworthy.*
— Keith Whitaker

Contents

Acknowledgments

As authors, we would like to acknowledge the colleagues, clients, friends, and family members with whom we have discussed the challenges and the opportunities inherent in family trusts. Thank you all. In particular, we would like to thank the following colleagues who took the time to read this book in manuscript and offer their comments: Patricia Angus, Tim Belber, Tim Brown, Paul Cameron, Greg Curtis, Mary Duke, John Duncan, Bryan Dunn, Rick Fogg, George Harris, Barbara Hauser, Steven Hoch, Holly Isdale, Dennis Jaffe, Don Kozuscko, Isabel Miranda, Miles Padgett, Ellen Perry, Scott Peppet, Christian Stewart, John A. Warnick, and Scott Winget. Bill Messinger earned our gratitude for his contribution to the interview on trusts and addiction in Chapter 15 and the model language regarding addiction found in Appendix 2. Similar thanks go to Rick Fogg for the sample legacy letter found in Appendix 1. We are grateful to Vanderbilt University's Owen

Graduate School of Management for giving us the opportunity
to share early versions of some of the content and exercises found
in this book with a tremendous group of students in June 2015.
Our deep thanks and appreciation go to the Haynes Family
Foundation, the Hemera Foundation, the FRED Fund, and
other individual donors who have supported our research and
writing. Any insights found herein are the shared bounty of our
friends; any infelicities are our own.

Our writing has also benefited from our reading of many fine
works related to trusts, family wealth, and positive psychology.
Those that we quote from or reference directly in this book are
noted at the end of each chapter. For readers who would like to
delve deeper into these topics, rather than providing a static
bibliography here in *Family Trusts*, we have created a regularly
updated bibliography online. To access this bibliography, please
visit www.wisecounselresearch.org.

Foreword
Jay Hughes

In the 1980s Joanie Bronfman, Richard Bakal, and I began a journey that continues to this day. We sought to try to make the relationships among the creator of a trust, its trustee, and its beneficiary comprehensible to all and humane. We set out to determine and define the rules and responsibilities of these three functions, which together shape each trust's culture and structure—the combination of which my co-author Hartley Goldstone later defined as the "trustscape." The early results of our efforts appeared in 1997 in my book *Family Wealth: Keeping It in the Family* (Netwrx). Those results have, over the years, been improved upon by many, and they are taken to a much deeper level in this book.

In the late 1980s Peter White, Joanie Bronfman, Anne D'Andrea, and I convened what I believe was the first gathering exclusively of trust beneficiaries. We had found to our surprise in our professional practices that many beneficiaries felt their trusts were burdens, not blessings. We wondered why a trust, which seemed on its face to be such a benefit, seemed so often to turn out to be the opposite. When we decided to host this gathering, we invited 50 or more people expecting that 10 might accept. To our amazement all accepted. We thought, "What have we started?" On the day of the gathering all 50 or more invitees showed up. Early in the meeting we took a poll asking, "Do you feel that the trust or trusts of which you are a beneficiary are more a burden or a blessing?" Eighty percent of the group raised their hands for "burden," 10 percent for "blessing," and the remainder could not decide between the two.

Perhaps many of you reading this book who are beneficiaries or trustees would not be surprised that in every poll of beneficiaries I have taken since—and I have taken many—the same percentages have consistently appeared: 80 percent or so feel their trusts are a burden, 10 percent a blessing, and the remainder are unsure. These results have given me a purpose ever since to see if my colleagues and I could change these percentages. This book is the result.

These percentages are a problem not only for beneficiaries. Changing these percentages is also critical to families' long-term flourishing. Among professionals it is well-known that by the third generation of a family around 90 percent of its financial wealth will likely be held in trust. Trusts represent, for almost all dynastic families, an overwhelmingly high proportion of ownership of their assets. Necessarily then these families' trust cultures and structures, their "trustscapes," and their beneficiary/trustee relations often determine whether the entropy of the "shirt sleeves to shirt sleeves" proverb overtakes them. Those of us in the field refer to this reality in the families we serve as "the trust wave."

So, 80 percent of trust beneficiaries declare that their trusts are burdens. And 90 percent of a dynastic family's financial wealth is in or will be in trust by the third generation. The combination of these facts underscores how important it will be to a families' flourishing that its trusts be blessings. It also underscores how important it is for us to learn from the small number of beneficiaries who feel that their trust is a blessing. That is what we have tried to do in this book.

Before proceeding, I would like to observe one other important demographic trend. The use of trusts continues to increase, not just for transfer tax planning but also for asset protection, reasons of probate, and, above all, control. This is true even in families without the wealth typically necessitating the use of trusts for transfer tax purposes (currently at well over $10 million). Within families with very significant or intergenerational wealth, beneficiaries may find themselves faced with trust distributions in their early 20s or younger. In many other families, as people live longer and longer lives, children or grandchildren may not begin receiving distributions until their middle- or later-middle-age, when their parents or grandparents pass away. However, this delay of the maturity of beneficial interests does not mean that the trusts in question do not exert a powerful force on these future beneficiaries' lives, especially if the trusts contain significant wealth. Nor is it impossible for trusts to enhance (or detract from) the lives of people in their 40s, 50s, or 60s. None of us is born an excellent beneficiary. To achieve this condition requires education and work, no matter how old you are. Indeed, insofar as it is generally harder to adapt to changes in later life, the delay of the maturity of beneficial interests may pose a growing threat to the successful use of trusts. It is a threat that we hope the practices described herein also help trustees and beneficiaries meet and overcome.

My co-authors and I are each committed to the question of human flourishing, especially in families of affinity seeking to practice seven generation thinking, that is, thinking that considers carefully the consequences of present-day actions on the people who will live seven generations later. These families preserve and grow their four qualitative capitals—spiritual, human, intellectual, and social—supported by their single quantitative capital, the financial. Such families often share a common core vision of what their members can be individually. These families' members decide, in their systems of joint decision making—their governance—to give up freedom to help enhance all other family members' journeys of happiness toward each member's own greater freedom. Such families tend to practice hastening slowly as they know they have to make just a few more seriously good decisions than bad over the next 150 years to succeed. They invest for the long term, with the intention that a later generation will harvest the hard won fruits of their labors. In contrast, we always worry when we see a family who thinks that it possesses only financial capital. Our experience, as well as history, advises that this belief is quite unlikely to lead to flourishing.

What have we learned about trusts and their functioning or failure from the families we advise? Why are so few trusts seen by their beneficiaries as blessings?

First, we have come to understand that our focus must start with the beneficiary, rather than with the trust creator or the trustee. Nearly all the writing in our field begins with planning for the trust creator's concerns over taxes, creditors, and control and then turns to the trustee's concerns over administration and investments. This focus on the trust creator easily follows from the fact that most professionals have the trust creator—and not the beneficiaries—as their paying client. It is the rarest of books and articles that treat the beneficiary side of the relationship and the distributive function. When they do often it is to disparage the beneficiary by discussing dependence, entitlement, bad marriages, addictions, or other failed developmental issues apparently caused by being a beneficiary. Clearly, this is a very disappointing point of view if the question of beneficiaries' flourishing is a critical goal.

In contrast, we came to see that beginning with the beneficiary and his or her responsibilities and goals might open new pathways to his or her flourishing. We first developed this line of thinking in a book that Keith Whitaker, Susan Massenzio, and I wrote called *The Cycle of the Gift* (Bloomberg, 2013). In that book we described a *gift* or a *transfer* as a meteor entering the atmosphere of the recipient to which he or she had to adapt. We asked, "What did the donor or transferor inspirit the meteor with?" Was it inspirited with love and a desire for the enhancement of the life of the recipient? Worry about the recipient's possible creditors? The transferor's tax concerns? The long-term control of the founder's dream? Was the meteor an Ozymandian monument requiring that the recipient genuflect for his or her beneficence? One can see immediately how much the grantor's intention for the beneficiary matters.

Next we looked at the question of the beneficiary's journey to individuation, which Keith and Susan and I discussed in our book *The Voice of the Rising Generation* (Bloomberg, 2014). And we reread Hartley Goldstone and Kathy Wiseman's book *TrustWorthy* (Trustscape LLC, 2012) with its wonderful stories of positive beneficiary/trustee relationships. We realized that a trust that has a deeply developed distributive function (and the distributive function is truly the key)—grounded in aiding the beneficiary's individuation, resilience, adaptability to meet life's ups and downs and capacity to bring his or her dreams to life—is the antidote against dependence, entitlement, cynicism, and addiction—addiction to alcohol or drugs as well as addiction to trust distributions.

We saw that one must begin with the recipient and work back through the system toward developing a highly functioning distributive methodology. From there one must work back to the quality of the trust creator's gift of love, seeking to enhance the life of the beneficiary and thus positively inspiriting that function. If one does so, then the likelihood of the beneficiary's declaring the trust a blessing is fundamentally improved. In turn, a beneficiary who counts his or her trust a blessing will likely want to assure that all family members with trusts are in similar positive situations now and for future generations. Such a person will likely add to family governance and flourishing as he or she seeks to give back to the family positive stories and share positive practices.

From this vantage point we were able to move toward the question of the nature of a trustee who would be committed to making the trust relationship with the beneficiary one that was mentoring, purposeful (thank you, John A. Warnick), generative, and fulfilling the high calling of regency (thank you, Patricia M. Angus). We recognized that nearly all beneficiary/trustee relationships are arranged marriages, even those in which the beneficiary has a voice in selecting the trustee. This is because the trustee is a part of a legal structure that requires him or her to obey the duty of impartiality, the duty of prudence, and to carry out multiple functions, very few of which are directly related to the well-being of the beneficiary, rather than to the protection of the trust and the trust creator's wishes. Essentially the trustee is married to the trust.

With this awareness it became clear to us that all too often the trustee is more concerned with the trust as a *structure* than with the *culture* that the trust creates. A culture that will succeed for the beneficiary begins with the trust creator's question: am I intending to make a gift of love and a gift that will enhance the beneficiaries' lives? Or am I seeking to make a transfer that solves my tax concerns, that keeps the beneficiaries' creditors from getting my money, and perhaps even creates a memorial to my dream, now embodied in an enterprise that I consider my true child and over which I seek through this trust to perpetuate my control? All these purposes are valid; but which ones lead and which ones follow will determine whether the trust is a blessing or a burden.

Often, a trustee cannot affirm for the beneficiary a set of positive goals and grow a positive trust culture. Instead, the beneficiary must live in a structure of relationships conditioned by a founder's goals that essentially disparage or ignore the beneficiary. For the beneficiary this is a negative culture, since the beneficiary's concerns will disappear in the endless details of the management of the structure. My thanks to Matthew Wesley for this insight, contained in his brilliant article, "Culture Eats Structure for Breakfast" (Wesley Group, 2015).

From all these sources and reflections we learned that a good way to diagnose whether the trust was growing a positive, dynamic culture or caught in the negative entropy of a static, suffocating structure was to ask this question: is the trust (guided by the trustee) making dynamic distributions that promote the beneficiary's growth and individuation, or is it making sterile, annuity-type payments that breed beneficiary dependence? The distributive function should really be the focus of mindful trustees and trust creators. Yet in most trusts it is stillborn; it is assumed that it will eventually become an annuity.

Looking at the generic trustscape today from the vantage point of the beneficiary we realized that most trusts aren't set up to grow excellent beneficiaries. Their cultures do everything but.

In contrast, we require new cultures and structures and systems that support them, if trusts are to be blessings and help long-term family flourishing. We need trust cultures that seek to grow excellent beneficiaries and structures and systems that support that happening. We need excellent beneficiaries who can in turn assure that their relationships with their trustees are excellent. We need trustees who grow the culture of trusts as gifts from trust creators rather than transfers. We need trust creators who are seriously counseled about what a trust can do and its consequences for another human being for whom it will always be a meteor. If the fundamental responsibility of each of us, when we touch another, is to do no harm—and it is—then how truly sad it is that 80 percent of trust beneficiaries count their trusts as burdens rather than blessings, especially when 90 percent of a family's financial capital will likely end up in trust. Clearly, the risk of harm is great.

A beneficiary who takes seriously his or her responsibilities will naturally function more effectively within the relationships the trust creates, as he or she comprehends and masters his or her role in the relationship rather than feeling burdened by it. Such beneficiaries are most likely to declare their trusts blessings. Those beneficiaries are also more likely to feel gratitude toward their trust creators and to say, "Not only was I not harmed, I was loved, and you blessed me." Those beneficiaries are more likely to say to their trustees, "Not only was I not harmed, my life was deeply enhanced by my relationship with you."

My colleagues Peter White, Joanie Bronfman, Richard Bakal, Anne D'Andrea, Susan Massenzio, Patricia M. Angus, John A. Warnick, Timothy Belber, Peter Karoff, Michael J. A. Smith, Sara Hamilton, Gail Cohen, Dennis Jaffe, Ellen Perry, Don Kozusko, Davidson Gordon, John Duncan, Christopher Armstrong, Joseph A. Field, Kathy Wiseman, Christian Stewart, Barbara Hauser, Charlotte Beyer, Gregory Curtis, Paul Cameron, Rick Fogg, Ken Polk, Ulrich Burkhard, George Harris, Stephen Hoch, Tim Brown, Rob Kaufold, Miles Padgett, Peter Evans, Robert Pritchard, Scott Peppet, Rob Kaufold, Juan Meyer, and many other pioneers in this work are beginning to unwrap this fraught question of the positive trustscape and the duties and responsibilities it engenders. For too long the "trust wave" has been leading families into entropy and the failed lives of beneficiaries that follow.

My co-authors, Keith and Hartley, and I are committed to bringing light into this area of unnecessary suffering so that no new beneficiary will ever have to wonder how he or she would answer the poll, and so that current beneficiaries may change their votes—all so the family systems of which they are members will flourish as they do.

As I have in my previous books I now ask each of you to pick up your staff, put on your round hats, drape your scallop shells around your necks and walk with Keith and Hartley and me through the chapters to come of this guide. Then, if it offers a way forward, walk with me on the journey to growing excellent beneficiaries so all trustscapes may flourish.

Bon Camino!

Namaste

James (Jay) E. Hughes Jr.

Preface

Hartley Goldstone

Somewhere this week—and likely on Twitter—some version of this headline will appear: *"Fallout from Settlement of Grandfather's Estate Splinters Family."*

In my case, it's also a haunting memory, affixed to a lively image: My grandfather Nathan is looking down from the hereafter. Tears are in his eyes. He slowly shakes his weary head in disbelief: "I never intended for this to happen."

The authors' hope, embodied in this book, is that your family will avoid the heartbreak of an estate plan gone very, very wrong.

What Can This Guide Do for You?

Until *Family Trusts*, no single book has offered families and their advisers field-tested ways to communicate about trusts; clarify intentions; develop excellent beneficiaries; and find, prepare, and transition excellent trustees.

This guide is for the family member who is serving or thinking of serving as trustee. Likewise, it can prove useful if you're an employee of a commercial trust company, private trust company, or family office, or a partner in a professional firm who is responsible for speaking with beneficiaries about qualitative rather than solely quantitative issues.

More broadly, this guide aims to help anyone else involved with family trusts, including (most importantly) beneficiaries as well as trust creators, trust protectors, trust committee members, and legal counsel.

We assume that you already have access to some degree of technical information along with excellent technical advisers. We won't be spending much time on taxes, the latest regulations, jurisdictional issues, and the whole host of other specialized topics that change from year to year.

What remains is the focus of the guide: the enduring work of boosting the quality of the relationships among those connected by trusts.

From Positive Stories to Action Steps

Years ago, I left the practice of law to accept a senior trust officer position. It was great to be thrust into the midst of families, especially trust creators and beneficiaries, wrestling with a kaleidoscope of dilemmas and opportunities. And what a change: suddenly I was administering trusts similar to those that I had formerly taken part in creating.

Imagine my surprise to see the reality of "bulletproof" plans being undone by the day-to-day actuality of family members interacting with me and with one another.

It was a daily effort to square the language of trust instruments with the life situation of beneficiaries. Legal skills obviously came in handy. But I was also glad for the time spent—this was before law school—on the staff of a social services agency, where I had helped people sort through challenges, some of which were full-blown crises.

Most of the correspondence I received was from beneficiaries requesting funds. The lively conversations that ensued often provided an opening for us to deepen our relationship. These distribution-related conversations were where opportunities for mentoring and thoughtful give-and-take about broader issues arose. I might ask something along the lines of: "What do you hope to accomplish by your request?" and then "Why is that important to you?" If it looked like I'd have to decline the request, we'd examine the goal and brainstorm alternate ways of achieving a good result without assistance from the trust.

Over time, my enthusiasm for trust administration faded. This change was not sudden, and no one event, family drama or internal policy shift caused me to lose hope; it was more a case of constant slippage. During a decade of administering trusts, and a second decade advising clients of a multifamily office, I saw my profession transform.

Local trust companies were swallowed up by ever-larger financial institutions. Centralized authority, standardized procedures, and short-term risk avoidance—important considerations, of course—chipped away at the traditional personal approach.

This way of administering trusts felt less and less effective and less and less satisfying. I left the institutional trust world to establish a consulting practice in 2009. If I ever doubted it, it was now emphatically clear that, because they are basic to family flourishing, successful trust relationships can't be handled like conventional "assets." One has to zero in on the qualitative work with whole-hearted purpose. Through writing, keynotes, workshops, and taking on related projects, I began translating what I had learned (and continue to learn) about flourishing trust relationships.

Over the years, I had played a part in many life-affirming stories where trusts made a lasting positive difference. These stories—counterpoints to all the nightmarish tales—stuck in my mind. In 2010, I launched the Beneficiary and Trustee Positive Story Project. At Jay's excellent suggestion, Kathy Wiseman joined the endeavor. We went to the source—beneficiaries, trustees, and their advisers—

asking them for positive stories about moments in time when relationships between trustees and beneficiaries worked well.

Relationships have their ups and downs. But what interested us were stories about the up times, even when they began with a down development—stories that showed strengths and evolution, perhaps a story about overcoming a challenge.

The project led to the October 2012 publication of a collection of the positive stories in *TrustWorthy—New Angles on Trusts from Beneficiaries and Trustees*.[1]

People loved the stories, because stories allow readers to get a feel for "how other families are handling it." Still, it's one thing to paint a picture of positive outcomes; it's quite another to help people achieve that type of outcome for themselves.

Our aim in *Family Trusts* is to help readers amplify their useful stories and reframe unhelpful ones. The method is to bring ideas to life through proven exercises for readers to try, questions carefully designed to stimulate new thinking, and illustrative stories that can help readers adapt this material to their own lives and practices. Together we will transform that relationship.

Everyone working with trusts recognizes the core challenge: the fear shared by parents and grandparents, *How can we help our children and grandchildren flourish rather than create "trust fund babies"?* This fear leads to delaying communication, secrets, and missed opportunities, and therefore fulfills itself: poorly prepared beneficiaries perform poorly.

In the face of this fear, a good trustee, an enlightened adviser, or a determined beneficiary can make all the difference.

We've seen lives transformed when both trustee and beneficiary stop viewing the trust that binds them together as a burden—and begin to view that very same trust as a resource to support the beneficiary's life purpose.

I'm a storyteller. So the best way I know to make this point is not to describe it, but to "show it" with a fable, with which I'll close this preface:

A Fable of Family Trusts

Part One

Grandma and Grandpa have accumulated financial wealth. So they make an appointment with a lawyer to create an estate plan.

In the days leading up to the appointment, nights are sleepless for Grandma and Grandpa. They are worried that their wealth will create "trust fund babies."

The day of the appointment arrives.

When Grandma and Grandpa enter the lawyer's office, a transformation happens.

Grandma and Grandpa are no longer "Grandma and Grandpa." They have been transformed into "clients."

The clients leave the lawyer's office with a bulletproof estate plan that protects against taxes, creditors, spendthrifts, and bad marriages.

On the way home, they reemerge as Grandma and Grandpa. They are still worried about creating trust fund babies.

Part Two

Grandson and Granddaughter love, and in turn are loved by, Grandma and Grandpa.

Grandson and Granddaughter are very sad when Grandma and Grandpa die.

The lawyer meets with Grandson and Granddaughter to explain his clients' estate plan.

Grandson and Granddaughter learn that Grandma and Grandpa created trusts for them.

But it becomes clear rather quickly that Grandson and Granddaughter's trusts are really best understood as "tax strategies."

The incidental beneficiaries of these tax strategies are very confused when they leave the lawyer's office.

Part Three

Grandson and Granddaughter meet with their trustee. The trustee is wise.

The trustee explains: "The lawyer created an estate plan for your grandparents that is first and foremost a legal relationship—one that only happens to involve human beings."

He continues: "Together, we will transform that legal relationship into a blossoming human relationship—a relationship among us that only happens to take place in a legal environment."

Prequel to the Fable

The trustee was not always wise. When he started out, like many trustees, he thought his job was to administer a legal relationship. He had his compliance manual, his audits, and his policies and procedures.

He wondered to himself why the beneficiaries he served were so unhappy. He knew that this was not what trust creators would have wanted for their loved ones.

One day he decided that "from today forth, I will administer trusts in a way that will enhance the lives of beneficiaries. The trust will be a resource to help them reach their potential, at whatever level their potential happens to be. . . ."

The authors, along with colleagues who share a similar outlook, have seen versions of this "fable" come to life, now and then, here and there. It always comes down to someone saying, "Let's take this legal relationship that only happens to involve human beings, and turn it into a human relationship that happens to take place in a legal environment." We're here to make the case—to you and yours—for the practical wisdom of this insight.

There's much at stake for our clients and their families—a good deal more than preservation of financial assets.

Hartley Goldstone

Note

1. Goldstone and Wiseman, *TrustWorthy—New Angles on Trusts from Beneficiaries and Trustees*. Trustscape LLC (2012).

Introduction

Keith Whitaker

Many years ago a member of my family asked me to serve as a trustee for a personal trust she had established. I agreed without much thought. It felt like a *pro forma* sort of thing: a document needed signing, and I was willing to sign it.

I had a lot to learn.

In the years since, I have served, paid and unpaid, as a trustee of many personal and charitable trusts as well as a director of or adviser to foundation boards, business boards, and private trust companies, for my family and for others. I have seen the great good that trusts can do, and the great harm. I have had the pleasure of working with generous grantors and grateful beneficiaries. I have had the displeasure of dealing with lawsuits over trusts that have torn apart families and friendships.

Along the way I have learned a great deal from other trustees, beneficiaries, and numerous advisers. One thing I learned is that my initial experience was not unusual. Few people begin service as a trustee with much clarity about what it entails. Most trustees begin as I did, wishing to do a favor for a family member or friend, unaware of the complexities and the opportunities that trusteeship brings with it.

For such trustees, the standard handbooks in the field— *Loring & Rounds* or *The Third Restatement of Trusts*—are amazingly rich but often too specialized. Coursework, such as that offered through the American Bankers Association, can help. But there has been no truly practical resource for the great majority of individual trustees.

Hartley, Jay, and I wrote this book to benefit any member of the "trustscape" (as explained in Part One) who finds him- or herself in a situation similar to mine those many years ago. You, our readers, are trustees, would-be trustees, beneficiaries, trust creators, or advisers who are conscientious and want to do the right thing. You may or may not have legal or investment expertise, but even if you do, you realize that your expertise may not completely prepare you for living with a trust. Most importantly, you recognize that your goal is to deal with that trust not only *correctly* (that is, in compliance with law and regulation) but above all *well*, namely, for the true good of all the people affected by it.

In writing this introduction and serving as a trustee, I have been guided by the belief that trusteeship is far more than a matter of administration. Even if unpaid, it is a *noble profession*. It is similar in this way to the noble professions of medicine, law, teaching, and the clergy. This means that even if a trustee performs his or her duties only a few hours a week or month, still, in those few hours, he or she is serving in a tradition that stretches back centuries and that has an inner worth of its own.

Principles

The rest of this introduction will say a few words about the principles that underlie the noble profession of trusteeship; it is meant to inform trustees, beneficiaries, and trust creators. It will also connect these principles and thoughts to the chapters and sections of the book that follows. In the main body of the book, Hartley, Jay, and I will outline practices and activities by which members of the "trustscape" can put these principles to work. If you would like to skip right to the practices, please feel free to jump to Chapter 1. If you would like to have a better understanding of our principles, then read on.

The five principles discussed here do not replace the traditional duties of the trustee, such as prudence, care, impartiality, and so on. Instead, what I have sought to do is to uncover some of the aspects of what we have elsewhere called the "fiduciary character" that makes any individual trustee the type of person who will fulfill these duties.[1] What trusteeship looks like will vary from time to time, place to place, and situation to situation. What makes up its core persists over time, place, and situation to give shape to the work amid changing circumstances.

1. First, Do No Harm

This is the first principle of every noble profession. Doctors swear it in the Hippocratic Oath. Lawyers, teachers, and the clergy have their own versions, spoken or unspoken.

This principle reminds us that trusts and trustees can do harm. Trustees have an intimate relationship with the other parties to a trust. We see confidential financial statements. Depending on the circumstances, we may be privy to confidential personal information regarding health, drug use, or other private behavior. Not honoring this "trust behind the trust" smashes the relationship to bits.

Sometimes doing harm takes on more subtle forms than exposing confidential information. Many trustees find themselves beset with "trust fund babies," that is, beneficiaries who live without work or purpose, dependent on their distributions. Is money the problem, "the root of all evil"? Or is family dysfunction the cause? Both may have a part to play. But the most common sort of trusteeship—tight-lipped, communicating only the bare necessities, winnowing down our relationship with beneficiaries to an annual letter along with the distribution checks—may also be a cause. The flip side of paternalism is infantilization. If we treat adults like children, it should be no surprise that we produce childish adults.

Not doing harm requires constant vigilance. That is why throughout this book, especially in Part Three, we emphasize practical ways that trustees and beneficiaries can develop strong relationships aimed at beneficiaries' growth.

After all, trusts and trustees can also do much good. The decisive difference lies in intention. Doing no harm is the first expression of what the Buddha called "right understanding," the understanding or view that sees the whole, accepts the whole, and then seeks to ease suffering.

Part of this right understanding is recognizing one's own boundaries. It is tempting, when one has been entrusted with perhaps millions of dollars, to believe that one can do it all. As the old Yiddish saying quips, "When you have money in your pocket, you're smart, you're handsome—and you sing well, too." In contrast, wise trustees do not fall prey to that temptation. They spend time and money to get the best advice that they can, whether around investments, law, taxes, communication, or human relations.

As Hartley and Jay have said, most trusts are proposed as expert solutions to the problem of minimizing gift, estate, or income taxes. In other words, most trusts aim at a *quantitative* goal. But if the trust exists for any period of time—and particularly if it does succeed at its quantitative goal—it will have an

immense *qualitative* effect on the lives of the grantor and beneficiaries. This qualitative side of the trust is almost never discussed
at its inception and often receives little attention during the trust's
life.

As a result, it often falls to the enlightened trustee or adviser
to be aware of and to foster the qualitative aspects in a positive
direction. To do this work, it can help to begin by recognizing
that the true capital placed in trust includes the human, social, and
intellectual—as well as financial—capitals embedded in the trust
relationship. This recognition then leads to asking, "Will this
distribution help the beneficiary add to his or her growth or
experience in life, his or her human capital? Will it help the
beneficiary connect with others in a meaningful way, thereby
increasing his or her social capital? Will it add to the beneficiary's
knowledge or skills, his or her intellectual capital?" This orientation to human capital is what we hope to achieve in Part One of
this book. We then take that orientation squarely into the
distributive function of trusts in Part Four.

2. Fidelity

Trustworthiness is more than not doing harm. It rests on solidity
of character, on standing by your word, on "ringing true" when
tested. That is *fidelity*, the core virtue of a trustee.

Although a servant may be faithful, fidelity is not servitude.
An agent serves. But a trustee is a principal, not an agent. If you
have asked someone to serve as trustee merely to do your
bidding, then you are not really looking for a trustee; you are
looking for an agent. The same goes if you are a beneficiary who
thinks that your wish should be the trustee's command.

Trustees owe their fidelity not only to the trust creator or to
the beneficiary or to themselves but to the trust—that is, the trust
relationship. This is a crucial point. Sometimes trustees will say that
they owe their fidelity to the trust *document*: "I will do only what's

permitted within the four corners of the document." The document is no doubt of great importance. But it is of importance because it has an impact on the lives of people.

Fidelity is not an easy path. Often, the more comfortable route is to become the agent of the trust creator or a beneficiary. Fidelity means recognizing and resisting these temptations. One way that I think of fidelity is that my role, as trustee, is not just to speak for the trust creator or just to listen to the beneficiary (though both of those activities are very important) but, above all, to keep alive the spirit of the gift. I owe my fidelity to the gift and the relationships it creates rather than only to the giver or only to the recipient.

What I mean by "the spirit of the gift" is a topic that goes beyond the confines of this introduction. My co-authors and I discuss it much more fully in our *Cycle of the Gift: Family Wealth and Wisdom* (New York: Bloomberg, 2013). Put simply, every true gift contains much more than the material "stuff" that is transferred. It contains spirit. Sometimes that spirit expresses expectations around work or education; sometimes it has to do with a vision of entrepreneurship; sometimes it concerns family life and relationships. The spirit of the gift may be expressed, in words or in writings, or it may be unspoken but felt. In any case, it holds great power for the giver and the recipient. As the Roman philosopher Seneca wrote 2,000 years ago, "As a gift is given, so shall it be received." If there is no spirit in a gift, then we call it a "transfer," and in such cases it is not surprising if the recipient finds the gift to be a lifeless or even life-draining force. Most of the gifts that lead to the "horror stories" told about "trust fund babies" are not gifts with spirit; they are transfers.

A trustee's fidelity expresses itself in its highest form in identifying, fostering, and keeping alive the spirit of the gift. There are various ways of doing so. It may mean helping the trust creator write down or record his or her wishes for the trust. It may mean trying to piece together those wishes, values, or philosophy after the grantor has passed away, in the form of a "preamble," as we discuss in Chapter 10. It may mean finding ways regularly to remind the beneficiaries of those values through individual or family meetings. It may also mean listening to the beneficiaries and working with them to figure out how to integrate the spirit of the gift meaningfully into their own lives. It is all the more important to take these steps if a trustee finds him- or herself entrusted with spiritless trusts—that is, trusts that embody transfers, set up solely with a view toward tax savings.

Ideally, the work of fidelity starts before the ink dries on a trust agreement. The practice of our co-author Jay Hughes is a case in point. For a decade before he retired from the active practice of law, Jay would always insist that anyone who asked him to write a trust would include at the beginning of the document these two lines: "This trust is a gift of love. It exists to enhance the lives of the beneficiaries." Jay's fidelity to his clients validated the fidelity of the future trustees of these trusts.

3. Regency

A regent rules while a young king or queen is still coming to maturity. It is a position of great honor and trust. It sounds quite grand or even grandiose.

But in the context of trusts, *regency* comes down to a less grand but very important point: that the trustee shall manage the trust relationship in such a way that when the beneficiary comes to maturity the trustee *could* dissolve the trust and hand over the assets in full faith that the beneficiary would use them well.

Regency aims at a qualitative goal: the beneficiary's maturity and independence. The regent's goal is not to grow the trust assets to be as large as possible. It is to help grow the lives of the beneficiaries, so that they become mature human beings, able to integrate the trust assets into a flourishing life.

If this sounds like a tall order, it is because it is. Much of the rest of this book, particularly Parts Three and Four, is devoted to describing practices that trustees, beneficiaries, and trust creators can use or establish in order to increase the probability that the family will succeed at this task—for it is possible to succeed.

But it is also important to acknowledge the obstacles to success. As my co-authors and I discuss in our book, *Voice of the Rising Generation: Family Wealth and Wisdom* (New York: Bloomberg, 2014), significant wealth often acts as a sort of "black hole," which can crush the dreams and aspirations of younger members of a family. Trusts are perhaps the most common means by which the black hole does its work. How easy it can be not to learn about yourself, not to take chances, not to discover and pursue your dreams, not to grow, if every month a sizable distribution lands in your bank account with no guidance and no spirit!

Faithful trustees-regents will seek ways to help beneficiaries mature and above all individuate, that is, discover and pursue their own dreams, thereby developing their own, individual personhood. The point, here, is in the intention. The principle of regency comes down to the intention to grow great beneficiaries, people to whom you *could* distribute all the assets, with a good conscience.

Regency contains within it the virtue of humility. It is an immense task—to grow a great human being. As any parent knows, it is a deeply humbling one. Most of us find it challenging to live our own lives well, much less help someone else do so.

This humble work is made only more challenging when pursued within the legal, "unnatural" landscape of a trust. The regent must look for ways to "deconstruct" that unnatural relationship and connect with the beneficiaries on a human level. As one wise trustee I knew used to put it, "I always look for ways to get to around that desk, over to the beneficiary's side." Again, many of the practices described in the rest of this volume are designed to help trustees make precisely this transition.

Pursued this way, regency allows the trustee to enact what the medieval Jewish philosopher Maimonides described as the highest rung on the "ladder" of giving. Maimonides offers this description in the context of discussing charity, but his words apply equally well to giving within families or serving as trustee. Maimonides describes several rungs on the ladder, starting near to the ground with giving that is forced or grudging, and moving upward to giving that has "strings attached." On the higher end of the ladder are gifts made anonymously, so that the recipient does not know who benefited him or her, and gifts in which the giver does not know who he or she benefited.

But the highest rung on the ladder, he says, is "when the giver reaches out a hand and, face-to-face, forms a partnership with the recipient." There is no hiding, no shame or embarrassment in this exchange. The two parties are face-to-face, hand-in-hand, as equal human beings. The gift is not a piece of property; it is the creation of a partnership. This is the moment that the trustee-regent strives for.

4. Discernment

The principle of *discernment* is closely related to some of the traditional duties of the trustee. A trustee is expected to exercise a "sound discretion" and model him- or herself on others of "prudence, discretion, and intelligence."[2] Also, more and more often today, attorneys are recommending that trust creators set up trusts that give the trustee "absolute discretion" to make distributions, thereby thwarting creditors or beneficiaries who want to get their hands on the trust principal or income.

Discernment is the basis for discretion. It is the habit of sifting the evidence. If a beneficiary requests a discretionary distribution, say, for a new car or a down payment on a house, the trustee must discern the reasons for and against the distribution. He or she must sift the evidence that the beneficiary presents as well as the possible consequences for the trust, the beneficiary, and other beneficiaries. (For more on discretionary distributions, see Chapter 14.) Discretion is the product of the habit of discernment.[3]

But discernment goes far beyond its application to discretionary distributions. It plays a part in the very process of accepting a trusteeship. Discernment requires asking yourself: Does this trust express the spirit of a gift? Am I able to serve in the role of keeping that spirit alive? Do I have the skills and knowledge requisite to truly help the parties to this trust relationship? Do I have the time and interest to apply those skills? Am I ready to go on a journey with these grantors and these beneficiaries? If so, what resources will I need to serve faithfully, as a regent, and *do no harm*? These are just some of the questions that enter in the process of acceptance, as we discuss in Chapter 9.

Discernment is also something that the wise trustee seeks to foster in the other parties to the trust. Even before a trust agreement is settled, a wise trust creator will go through a process of discernment in order to clarify and express the spirit of his or her gift. A discerning trustee will encourage this process. Also, the trustee's discernment can have a positive effect on beneficiaries. Making sure that beneficiaries understand the process of discernment that you use in managing the trust can lead them to internalize this process in their requests for information or distributions.

The work of regency rests upon discernment. Sometimes a trustee can act in a way similar to the "spiritual director" that St. Ignatius describes in his classic book on the discernment of spirits and of God's will.[4] As we describe in Chapter 14, wise trustees seek to serve as a counterbalance to beneficiaries' positions, not to thwart beneficiaries but rather to get them to reflect more deeply on who they are and what they want. For a beneficiary who is shy and reluctant to ask questions, the discerning trustee may be more engaging, open, and welcoming. For a beneficiary who looks like he is getting sucked into the "black hole" of measuring his own worth by the trust's assets, the discerning trustee may try to help him focus on his own goals, dreams, and opportunities for growth, apart from the money.

Another way that a trustee or, more likely, a trust protector can have a positive effect is on the trust "system" as a whole. It takes time, humility, and great delicacy, but a discerning trust protector can, in some situations, be exactly the right person to handle the "judicial" function within a family, that is, the function of resolving conflicts such as between the trustee and beneficiary. This work entails helping both parties undergo a discernment process. Such discernment is truly the place where the trust protector becomes a family elder. In family after family that I have seen, especially in families that are in their third generation or beyond of living with wealth, there is perhaps no one but the elder-protector who stands in the position of trust and authority requisite to do such work. We have much more to say on this exciting and powerful role in Part Four.

5. Courage

Courage bears a direct relation to everyone involved in the trustscape. It takes courage to create a trust. It takes courage to take on the task of integrating a trust effectively into your life as a beneficiary. And it certainly takes courage to serve as a trustee, trust protector, or trust adviser.

All these roles require going on a journey with a family over many years. It demands getting to know them as human beings, with all the fine qualities and not-so-fine qualities that we all have. It requires accepting that this journey will have its ups and downs and, as in any journey, accepting the role that chance may play.

Courage, like discernment, is also a principle that members of the trustscape can extend to the system itself. In this sense, it is *encouragement*. A courageous adviser or trustee can encourage a trust creator to think through the spirit of her gift and then communicate it clearly and openly. The trustee's encouragement can make even more of a difference for beneficiaries. Here, the courageous trustee can encourage them to envision their aspirations and make them real. He or she can help them pursue their education, make connections, and explore different avenues of work. The courageous trustee will also make sure that money does not swamp those dreams. Such a trustee may, at times, *not* make distributions if those distributions would undermine the beneficiaries' journey. It is easier to write a check or give in to a demand. It is harder and takes courage to say, "No, but . . ." and then show a way forward that does not depend on money. My experience is that even frustrated beneficiaries appreciate such courage, and that it helps them find the courage within themselves to continue to struggle and to rise on their own.

As already mentioned, the wise trustee will always temper his or her principles, including courage, with humility. One of the most courageous things you can do is to recognize what is within your power and what is not, and when to let go. Some of these situations we describe in Chapter 17, on transitions.

Families change over time, sometimes drifting apart and losing touch. But no family has a natural life span. When a family dissolves is its choice. It does not have to be today or tomorrow or next year or decade. Trusts can be an agent for family stability and growth rather than dissolution. This is one message that we hope all members of the trustscape hear from this book. It is a message of great hope and solace for family members who very often feel misgiving about the likely effects of significant wealth in their children or grandchildren's lives. Acting on this message of hope takes courage. But this courage can reap qualitative dividends for a family for years to come.

These five principles—do no harm, fidelity, regency, discernment, and courage—are the foundation of wise trusteeship and indeed of a sound trustscape. I do not offer them as a yardstick by which to judge yourself. Instead, I hope that they prompt your reflection on your own place in the trustscape and your own strengths and the ways you best apply those strengths to helping yourself and others. A noble profession is not made up of rules handed down from above. It consists of a way of life. It is your privilege to make that way your own.

Notes

1. See Hartley Goldstone, Scotty McLennan, and Keith Whitaker, "The Moral Core of Trusteeship: How to Develop Fiduciary Character." *Trusts & Estates* (May 2013), 49–52.

2. These classic statements come from a foundational decision in trust law, *Harvard College v. Amory*, 9 Pick. (26 Mass.) 446, 461 (Mass. 1830).

3. For much more on discernment, see my *Wealth and the Will of God: Discerning the Use of Riches in the Service of Ultimate Purpose*, with Paul Schervish (Bloomington: Indiana University Press, 2010).

4. St. Ignatius, *Spiritual Exercises*, annotations 13–15.

Part One

INTRODUCING THE TRUSTSCAPE

Chapter 1

Navigation Works Better When You Have a Destination in Mind

Here's a question that can lead to a world of good. Whether you're a trust creator, trustee, or beneficiary, ask yourself: "What's the single most important reason for the existence of my trust?" Not the sole reason, and not the first one that likely comes to mind, but the one that, upon reflection, takes precedence over any of the others—what is that reason?

Here is a second question that is more future focused: "What's the most important outcome I'd like my trust to accomplish?" Your answers amount to your vision of the "destination." Having a clear destination in mind will influence just about every trust-related decision.

With nearly all our client families, we suggest this thought as the most important reason for creating a trust: To make a gift that promotes growth and thereby lays the groundwork for the beneficiary's true *freedom*. This is in contrast to a mere transfer of assets, which tends to siphon off energy and lead to entitlement.[1]

> The single most important reason for creating a trust is to make a gift that promotes the beneficiary's true freedom.

If you use "freedom" as a standard, the ongoing test becomes whether the existence of the trust—and the relationships created by the trust—enhances rather than diminishes the lives of the beneficiaries. *Enhance* has various meanings, but all of them are positive. Specifically, we mean the type of *enhancement* that helps beneficiaries mature and come to know and pursue their own aspirations.

> Will the existence of this trust, and the relationships created or altered by this trust, enhance the lives of the beneficiaries?

We further suggest that advancing the goal of life enhancement requires moving toward a series of "right" relationships between and among those touched by the trust. In our view, getting these relationships right often means asking different questions from the usual.

What types of inquiry work best? When getting to know a brand new beneficiary, a seasoned trustee might have thoughts like these to offer to that beneficiary:

- This type of relationship is altogether new to you. Although I've been a trustee for many other beneficiaries, our relationship is new and unique to me, as well. So what do you think are some solid steps for us to take toward becoming colleagues in a reciprocal relationship? If I am to mentor you, how would you like to be mentored?
- How can our relationship generate positive energy for each of us, rather than take energy away or make either or both of us feel like we're "mired in quicksand"?
- How can our relationship help to bring your aspirations to life? Aspirations for your family or community, and especially for your individual growth?

Or, suppose a beneficiary is dissatisfied with his or her relationship with the trustee. This inquiry is more self-directed:

- What have I (the beneficiary) contributed to our falling out?
- What's a step—no matter how small—I might take toward getting us back into "right" relationship?
- Who do I know who might help me think this situation through?

Decades of experiencing both right relationships and those that are off track have led the authors to conclude that the highest duty of both trustee and beneficiary is to tackle this question: If the trust should end and the assets be distributed to the beneficiary tomorrow, would the beneficiary have the knowledge, the maturity, and the competency to receive and steward the funds well?

It follows that the trustee's highest duty is to prepare the beneficiary to take that event in stride. And the corollary: the beneficiary's highest duty is to prepare him- or herself.

> If the trust should end and the assets be distributed to the beneficiary tomorrow, would the beneficiary have the knowledge, the maturity, and the competency to receive and steward the funds well?

While the task of preparing someone else or preparing oneself to receive assets is very real, the *distribution* envisioned is hypothetical. It exists as a thought experiment. We want beneficiaries to develop the skills and maturity to integrate the distribution well, not because the distribution will likely take place (it probably won't), but because those skills and maturity are also requisite to living well itself.

Beyond the Thought Experiment

For some families, *termination* and distribution are more than a thought experiment. These families are wrestling with how to approach impending distributions of large sums—some of which have been held in trust for generations.

Let us explain. As 2012 came to a close, business was booming for tax lawyers. There was a rush to create new trusts, driven by fear: Would the amount one could pass from one generation to the next, and do so tax free, be dramatically reduced? Not wishing to take that chance, many trusts were cobbled together as the clock ticked toward midnight on December 31.

Although the timing had an element of drama, the motivation was not new.

Trusts, like wines, have "vintage" years. During a vintage year, the creation of a large number of trusts is triggered by fiscal events (tax law changes) or nontax legal events (e.g., the elimination of the Rule Against Perpetuities). Dynastic families also have their own vintage years driven by family circumstances.

The significance is that some families will have batches of trusts "maturing" (either terminating or being transformed) at roughly the same time.

Some vintage years include:

1931: Many trusts were created in anticipation of 1932, when the top estate tax rate jumped from 20 percent to 45 percent and the estate tax exemption dropped from $100,000 to $50,000.

1933: Trusts created in anticipation of 1934, when the maximum estate tax rate increased to 60 percent.

1934: Another vintage year in anticipation of the maximum estate tax rate increasing to 70 percent and estate tax exemption decreasing to $40,000.

Trusts created during the 1930s are maturing now—all these decades later—due to deaths of the trusts' measuring lives (people now in their 80s), which means that many families have to prepare beneficiaries to receive trust assets. In these families—for the first time in generations—beneficiaries will receive substantial distributions as trusts terminate.

This is why the duty to help prepare beneficiaries to integrate distributions well is more urgent than just a thought experiment.

Of course, we are writing this book not only for families facing the termination of "vintage" trusts from the 1930s. There are many other reasons that a family may face a trust termination. (Apart from more common reasons, it is always possible that Congress could raise the income tax on trusts significantly or pass other legislation unfriendly to trusts. In that event, families would be tempted to look into unwinding existing trusts.) And even if you are not facing a termination now, the question of, "What would we do if we had to terminate this trust?" can help focus attention on the way that your family is handling current distributions. As we will see, the distributive function is really the heart of trusts, and the determining factor as to whether trusts succeed or fail in growing the family's human capital.

Questions for Reflection

- What do you think are some valid reasons—the purpose and, to some extent, the destination—that should drive creation of a trust?
- What do you think should be the highest duties of the trustee and beneficiary?
- What other duties would you see as either complementary or even superior to these in your particular case?

Note

1. For more on the difference between "gifts" and "transfers," see James E. Hughes Jr., Susan E. Massenzio, and Keith Whitaker, *The Cycle of the Gift: Family Wealth & Wisdom* (New York: Bloomberg, 2013).

Chapter 2

The Trustscape

Now that you have had a chance to think about where you are heading, we'd like you to consider taking part in an unusual exercise, an exercise designed to begin to paint the picture of the environment within which your journey is taking place.

Our purpose in this exercise is to shift the focus in estate planning from legalistic structures like trusts and partnerships to a different center of attention—the relationships that are created among the people who are touched by the structures.

As the first step, remove a handful of coins from your pocket, or your purse. Hold those coins in your hand and examine them.

Notice the different sizes of the coins, the different colors. Can you also sense the differing weights? Look thoughtfully at the images. Some of the coins are new and shiny, some much older. One might even be "dinged up."

If you happen to be looking at an American penny, on the "head" side you'll notice a portrait of Abraham Lincoln. On the "tail" appears the motto: "E Pluribus Unum," which is Latin for "Out of Many, One." Not a bad motto for those related through trusts, for that matter.

Portraits on American coins picture people who are no longer living. Not so for British coins. Here you'll see coins depicting the queen. As for the euro, there are no portraits to be found. Every euro coin carries a common image on one side and a different motif selected by each member state on the other.

The coins of China—which invented paper money in the ninth century—picture beautiful irises and lotuses along with the inscription *zhongguo renmin yinhang*. In English, that's "People's Bank of China."

No matter your local currency, place the coins on top of a piece of white paper on a table or other surface in front of you. Choose one of them and imagine that the coin is you. Did you pick a large coin? A small one?

Now think of each of the other coins that are spread out on the paper as a different member of your family. If you are married, which coin is your spouse? Which coins are parents and grandparents, children and grandchildren, brothers, sisters, nieces, nephews, and cousins?

Next, move the coins around. Let them come to rest in ways that illuminate how family members are emotionally connected with one another. Which coins are grouped closely together? Which are farther apart? Are some coins on top of others? Are there any that you move to the far reaches of the table?

As you arrange and rearrange the coins, allow yourself to feel positive associations with some coins and negative emotions toward others.

Do you notice how these coins, which moments ago were nothing more than unremarkable bits of metal, are now infused with feelings?

Introducing Your Trustscape

Now, add some coins to your tableau. Go ahead and assign them to be your family's trusts, the trustees, and, if applicable, the trust protector and related advisers. Once again rearrange your coins to bring these added relationships into the picture.

Focus on the coins (people) that are linked by your trusts. These are the people, the trust documents, and the relationships that make up your *trustscape*. Like you did a few moments ago, take some time to notice the emotional connections. This time, focus on connections among you and those linked by your trusts. Take out a pencil and circle the coins and draw lines to represent the connections.

(By the way, we recognize that many families live amid multiple trusts. Some families we have worked with navigate dozens or even hundreds—and in a few cases, thousands—of trusts, not to mention family foundations or family limited partnerships. For simplicity's sake, in the rest of this book we often speak about a "trust," a "trustee," or a "beneficiary" in the singular. But we always have in mind that in reality many of our readers are dealing with systems of multiple trusts, trustees, and beneficiaries. That is one reason that the concept of the trust-scape is so helpful.)

When you are finished circling your coins and drawing your lines, step back and take a look at your tabletop tableau. It's all here: family, money, trusts—in both physical and emotional form, with a sense of the proportions as well, you'll have the complexity that defines the interrelationships. This is your trustscape.

The paper and ink of your trust documents—much like the coins—have a full-blown charge of emotions attached to them.

Most trustscapers would say that optimizing their trust-related relationships is best achieved through a deliberate process, rather than a random one. Yet the majority lack a "tabletop tableau" to sharpen focus and clarify direction.

Feel free to snap a picture of your tableau with your camera or smartphone and refer back to it often as you work your way through this guide. But keep in mind, like any living system, your trustscape will always be changing.

Questions for Reflection

- What most surprised you as you went through the coin exercise?
- What new insights did you gain?
- Does visualizing your family's estate plan as a tabletop tableau of relationships sharpen your focus?
- Where does the estate plan get the relationships right?
- Where does the estate plan get in the way?
- Where do you see resources and opportunities to build upon?

A Dynamic Tableau

You were just encouraged to move coins around a table top to visualize your trustscape. Whenever the coins came to rest, a snapshot was in order: "Here's what my trustscape looks like—as of this moment."

But in the real world no one person can control how the "coins" move. So we had best add depth and randomness to our visual display by introducing a second metaphor. Because of its dynamic and highly fluid nature, the trustscape in fact functions as a seascape.

A trustscape, like a seascape, has currents and cross-currents on the surface as well as below. Some days are sunny with clear sailing. On other days fog may roll in and squalls unexpectedly arise. Navigating either "scape" may at times feel enchanting and at other times hazardous.

In good weather, an inexperienced sailor may be able to navigate a placid lake without getting into too much trouble. When contemplating venturing out to sea, however, that same sailor would be well advised to first gain education and experience, or plan to bring along an able sailor.

Similarly, "trustscapers" must acquire the tools and know-how of skillful *navigation*.

Now imagine that you had the power to change your trustscape in ways that would strengthen relationships and improve people's lives. Move the coins accordingly. Add or subtract coins as necessary. Draw or redraw the relationship lines. And, when you're done, snap a picture of this, your *aspirational* trustscape. You can't control the wind or the weather, but at least this picture of your desired trustscape gives you a sense of where you'd like to sail.

Question for Reflection

- Who are your "able sailors" (mentors) to help you direct your keel deeper into the ocean? Chances are, you'll add to your list as this guide unfolds.

A Closing Exercise

Imagine you've finished your reading for today and have put this book down. You get on with doing the usual things you do, until it's time to go to bed. You are very tired, the household is quiet, and you fall into a deep and peaceful sleep.

You awaken and—lo and behold—you are able to see into the future. No matter how fantastical it always seemed, all your trust-related hopes and dreams are suddenly real. You think to yourself: "This trust really worked out!"

What clues do you notice that tell you of this success? What are people saying? What are they doing? What are they feeling?[1]

Better Yet . . .

Imagine how powerful the exercise would be if you were to do it again—this time as a group effort along with other members of your trustscape.

If you and the others are up for it, consider setting aside time to try the exercise together. See if you can hash out a collaborative vision of a successful trustscape. Where do you agree? Where do you lack consensus? How will this help bring your trusts to life?

Note

1. This "miracle" question is adapted from Steve de Shazer and Yvonne Dolan, *More than Miracles: The State of the Art of Solution-Focused Brief Therapy* (Binghamton, NY: Haworth Press, 2007). The miracle question is useful to help visualize a preferred future.

Chapter 3

Some Key Terms

In a book of this type, it helps to define some key terms. There is a danger in doing so, and of trying to be too specific, if author and reader alike get stuck in a single understanding of terminology. With these initial definitions in mind, as you go through the guide, develop your own, many-layered understanding of these and other terms.

Trustscape. As you experienced in the prior two chapters, the trustscape is a subsystem of the larger family system. The trustscape is populated by all those touched by trusts—the trust creator, the beneficiaries, the trustee, perhaps a trust protector and a trust committee, and each of their cadres of legal, financial, accounting, and other advisers. The denizens of a trustscape can collectively be referred to as *trustscapers.*

Trust. Trusts originated in the Middle Ages. Noblemen who went off to war or on long journeys knew that they might not survive to return home. So they asked someone they trusted—often it would be the local bishop—to look after their property. The owners instructed their trustees on how to manage the property and what to do with the property should word get back that they had died.

The nature of trusts—a trust creator transfers property to a trustee to manage on behalf of a beneficiary—hasn't changed much over the years.

The document that creates a trust may be a will or a trust agreement, but a trust is more than a piece of paper; it is the relationship among the creator, the trustee, and the beneficiary. Please see Chapter 5 for more on what trusts are.

Trust creator. The person who creates a trust often goes by names such as *grantor, settlor,* or even *donor.* We'll use the term *trust creator.* We explain why in Chapter 7.

Trustee. The trustee—one entrusted—is legal owner of property held by a trust. The trustee has a fiduciary duty to ignore his or her own interests and administer the property for the benefit of the beneficiary. As a result, although the legal *owner* of the trust property, the trustee does not usually enjoy the *use* of that property. We have more to say about trustees in Chapter 6.

Beneficiary. Rather than being the legal owner, the beneficiary has an "equitable" interest in the property owned by a trust. In this way, the beneficiary obtains use of the property without being its legal owner. If you are a beneficiary, the trust's money is not "your" money.

A "current" beneficiary has the right to receive distributions from the trust right now. A "contingent" beneficiary *may* have the right to receive distributions at some point in time, but only if some specified event occurs first. For example, the contingent beneficiary may be entitled to distributions following someone else's death. A "remainder" beneficiary (sometimes called a *remainderman*) receives whatever property is left in the trust (the "remainder") when the trust comes to an end.

You can read much more about beneficiaries in Chapter 7.

Trust protector. A trust protector may be given discretion to remove and replace trustees. A less obvious role, but one that's very important, is to help create, maintain, and regenerate the spirit of the gift in trust, especially when the trustee fails to do so. (For more on the "spirit of the gift" see the Introduction.) We discuss trust protectors and other trust advisers in Chapter 8.

Trust distributions. "Mandatory" distributions must take place, based on the language of the trust agreement. "Discretionary" distributions take place at the discretion or choice of the trustee. The trust document may provide that some mandatory distributions to the beneficiary are automatic (e.g., perhaps distribution of income). Other mandatory distributions may be scheduled (e.g., when a beneficiary reaches a certain age). The trustee is often given flexibility to make "discretionary" distributions for things such as support, health, and education. Trust distributions and the distribution process are the focus of Chapter 14 and Part Four. In many cases, a trust's distributive function is ignored until a beneficiary makes a request; one of our main goals in this book is to prompt serious and proactive thinking about the purpose and good use of the distributive function.

Principal and *income.* Principal refers to property owned by the trust. The trust property or principal may include stocks, bonds, cash, mutual funds, as well as real estate, intellectual property, or tangible property such as jewelry or cars. The trust's property (one hopes) generates income, such as interest, dividends, or rent.

Distribution Committee. The Distribution Committee is introduced for the first time in this guide. In some trustscapes, this committee is available to counsel the trustee regarding a beneficiary's requests for distributions of funds. You can learn much more about the distribution committee in Chapter 20 and in Appendix 3.

Office of the Beneficiary. Like the Distribution Committee, the Office of the Beneficiary is currently being developed and field-tested by a small number of families and is introduced here for the first time. The Office of the Beneficiary is made up of advisers selected and paid for by the beneficiary. The purpose of the Office of the Beneficiary is to mentor the beneficiary in the areas of trust administration, trust investing, and trust distributions. As with the distribution committee, we describe the office of the beneficiary at much more length in Chapter 20, as well as in the rest of Part Four.

Chapter 4

Know Your Narratives

The prior three chapters have introduced you to the trust-scape and to the question of where you may be trying to get to within that environment. It is tempting to move from this point quickly to the practicalities of building the trustee-beneficiary relationship or to the even more fundamental, informational business of who are the various players in the trustscape.

But before doing so, we want to spend one more moment on a basic matter of relationships: the orientation that we bring to these structures and roles.

Consider this scenario: A beneficiary who has never met her trustee before walks into the trustee's office for their first meeting. What's the agenda? In the beneficiary's mind, perhaps beyond one or two mechanical questions, her agenda is likely to get through the meeting. A certain amount of "jitters" is natural, and the specific goals, if they exist, are in the mind of the other person.

But that doesn't mean the trustee is in the most receptive state, either. This might be his 150th experience getting acquainted with a brand new "B." With such a rich database, any professional has coding mechanisms, some of which are subliminal.

Let's assume the beneficiary uses a phrase, or simply gives a look, that vaguely reminds the trustee about his or her all-time most vexing trust situation. In that case, two sets of "jitters" are at work. Tension automatically takes over on the part of the trustee, who would otherwise be doing his best to bring conscious professionalism to the early stages of this trustscape connection.

The point is that the qualities that, in the moment, we attach to an individual or a situation are subjective. Our personal experience, stories (or snippets of stories) from friends about their particular trustscapes, or perhaps even a fleeting memory or an overheard offhand comment are accessed—even when not consciously looked for.

The result is our "*narrative*" about the person or situation. Sometimes we get so caught up in our uniquely personal narratives that they seem like dependable truths. And our narratives, whether they happen to be positive or negative, may serve us well—or maybe not so well. It is particularly common for us to return to habitual narratives when we face moments of stress.

So it's no surprise that some beneficiaries believe that the problems in their lives are a reflection of certain "truths" about their trusts and trustees. They may assign labels: My trust is "restrictive" or "unjust." My trustees are "controlling" or "uninterested."

Trustees, in turn, may think of beneficiaries as "dys-functional" or "entitled," which just about guarantees uneasiness at the next meeting.

Given the power of these narratives, regardless of your age and status, we cannot overemphasize the importance of coming to grips with your own narratives about your distinctive trustscape.

To help you get started, here's an exercise we sometimes do in educational programs about family trusts.

Depends Where You're Sitting

Imagine a large round table. Seated around the table are family members of different generations, family advisers, trustees, and others who are touched in one way or another by the family's trusts.

Now imagine that at the center of the table is an oversized beach ball made up of different-colored panels. If asked to describe ball's color, one might say "red and white and yellow," or "blue and green and orange," or some other combination, depending on where each observer is seated.

Everyone at the table is describing the ball accurately from his or her vantage point—yet no two descriptions match. And the beach ball always remains the very same beach ball.

Now imagine that the beach ball is replaced by a trust instrument. The same people are at the table. Each describes the trust from his or her vantage point. Different descriptions, same trust.

The creator of the trust might say something that begins with: "I created this trust because . . ."

The attorney: "I drafted this legal document to protect against taxes, creditors, and . . ."

A trustee: "My most important duty as trustee is . . ."

One beneficiary: "This trust creates many problems for me because . . . "

Another beneficiary: "This trust is a blessing because . . ."

And so on.

Now it's your turn to speak. Imagine that the trust agreement sitting in the middle of the table is a trust that affects your life. How would you describe it? What would you say? What's your narrative about trusts? Even if you're a brand new trustee or beneficiary, you have one.

Pick and choose from among these questions to help you get started.

- Think of *positive assumptions* about the trust and, for that matter, about the others sitting around the table—what are these positive assumptions? Where did they come from? How do they serve you? Thought for thought, how do they stand up? Suppose you had more positive assumptions— what difference would that make? Where and how could you "try out" a few of those?

- *Negative assumptions*—what are they? Where did they come from? Do they serve you? If so, how? How credible are they? Name a time or two when a negative premise or scenario didn't prove out. What was happening that might have "flipped" that meeting or conversation?

A Thirst for Education

Sometimes narratives about others may get us caught up in a destructive way of thinking. Here's a situation related by a trust officer:

> James was part of a very wealthy family that had a family office. The head of the family office was the individual trustee, with a trust company as co-trustee. The head of the family office had a very long history with James that was quite negative. He did not trust James, he didn't like him, and James knew it.

James called me, the trust officer for the trust company, one day. He was in his late 30s at this point, living most of the time in Paris. He said, "I want to go back to school. I want to get a postgraduate degree at the Sorbonne. There is a program that I like very much, and it will take me about two years to complete. This will enable me to have a better life, and maybe I will become a teacher. I don't know what I want to do specifically, but this program will provide me with career choices I won't otherwise have. This is something I really want to do."

After I got off the phone with James, I then called the individual trustee and he said, "Absolutely not—I don't trust James. How do we know he is really going to use the money for that purpose?"

The problem the co-trustee had was that he couldn't conceive that James had changed.

I had a different take on James than the other trustee did. I really thought that he was serious in this endeavor. I did not know him as long as the other trustee, so there wasn't a negative history with me.[1]

James and his trustees worked out an arrangement that included checks and balances. James was indeed serious, completed his education, and moved on to the next stage of his life.

The point is that, if a particular narrative (positive or negative) serves us well, we can expand upon it. If not, we may be able to break loose of it. That's easy to say, but doing so requires deliberate effort. Our natural tendency is to resist change, especially of narratives that are longstanding.

Our friend Stephanie West Allen, a skilled mediator knowledgeable about neuroscience, suggests that we're more likely to embrace a new narrative if we:

- Are aware of our present narrative.
- Have an important reason to replace it.

- Make a decision to change it, and
- Are resolved to keep going in the face of resistance.

These additional questions should help you clarify your narratives.

If you are (or will be) a trustee:

- What positive assumptions do I have about myself as trustee? Where do they come from? How do these positive assumptions help me?
- And while I'm at it, what are some of my strengths and virtues?
- How can I bring my strengths and virtues into play in my role as trustee? What difference will that make to me? To the beneficiary?

And if you are a trustee who has been—and still may be—a beneficiary yourself:

- Can I recall a trustee who made a difference—a trustee who made me feel cared for and respected? Maybe someone who earned my trust over time? What told me that caring, respect, and trust was present? What benefit was it for me? For my trustee?
- How can I bring more of the good things that I myself have experienced as a beneficiary into my role as trustee?

If you are (or will be) a beneficiary:

- What am I saying, thinking, and feeling about being a beneficiary? About my trust? About my trustee? Where do these narratives come from?
- Do some of these narratives (positive or negative) serve me? If so, how do they serve me? What difference does that make?
- Would changing a narrative or two serve me better? If so, how? If I do change a particular narrative, what difference might that make? What's a step I can take now, no matter how small, to begin to make that change?

We have now oriented ourselves to the trustscape—the environment of people, structures, roles, and responsibilities that grow up quite naturally around a family trust. We have the help of some key terms, and we have had a chance to reflect on where we are trying to go and what assumptions we bring with us as we start out on the journey. In the next part of this book, we look more closely at some of the denizens of the trustscape with a view particularly to their roles and responsibilities. We will then move on to the practical work of building stronger relationships across the trustscape.

Note

1. Excerpt from "James Has a Thirst for Education," in *TrustWorthy*. © Trustscape LLC. Reprinted with permission.

Part Two

THE PLAYERS

Chapter 5

The Trust

I f you were to ask 100 trustscapers to describe a trust (and we have), about 60 might say it is some sort of vessel to receive and hold assets; another 30 would probably say it is a legal document or a tax strategy; and the rest wouldn't be sure. As we have seen, those 90 percent would be, for the most part, mistaken. A trust is properly viewed as a relationship among trust creators, trustees, and beneficiaries.

In this chapter, we take a *very* brief overview of the legal nature of this relationship. We'll have a lot more to say about the attendant emotional relationships throughout this guide.

A Short Description of a Long History

For centuries, the legal principles defining trust relationships arose from decisions made by courts, rather than from statutes passed by legislatures. Trust law has historically been judge-made law.

According to this legal tradition, a trust relationship requires several elements to exist: (a) the intent to create a trust, (b) a lawful purpose, (c) property that is titled to the trustee, and (d) an ascertainable beneficiary.

A trust creator must *intend* to create a trust relationship.[1] That's most often accomplished with the assistance of an attorney who drafts a written trust instrument. The language that creates the trust may be found within a will or in a separate trust agreement.

A trust creator may be motivated to create a trust for almost any lawful *purpose*. Common purposes "range from the avoidance of probate, to providing property management for those who cannot, ought not, or wish not to manage for themselves, to providing for limited and successive enjoyment of property over several generations, and including as well such objectives as the saving of taxes and the insulation of trust property from the claims of beneficiaries' creditors."[2]

The trust creator transfers *legal title* of property *to the trustee*. The types of property that may be received by the trustee are seemingly limitless:

- Personal residences including vacation homes.
- Personal property such as art, vehicles, jewelry, furniture, and generally, possessions other than real estate.
- Stocks and bonds (and more complex securities like derivatives and interests in private partnerships such as hedge funds).
- Investment real estate.
- Closely held businesses.
- Insurance policies.

The trustee manages the property *on behalf of the beneficiary*. The relationship between trustee and beneficiary is a *fiduciary relationship*. Think of the fiduciary relationship as one that imposes on the trustee duties of undivided loyalty and prudence.

Before proceeding, take a moment to notice what does *not* appear among these four legally required elements of a trust. There is no mention of a vessel or receptacle. There is no mention even of a document: a trust can sometimes come into being without written terms. (Obviously, it is much wiser to write those terms down.) And there is no mention of a trustee. Yes, a trustee is crucial. But a trust can exist without one. Sometimes a trustee resigns without appointing a new trustee in its place. In such cases the current beneficiaries may have to take action to elect a new trustee. The trust doesn't disappear if there is no trustee.

Now take a moment to notice what *does* appear among these four elements. The trust creator is present but only in the shadows, as the source of purpose, intent, and (probably), property. The only person who appears in the four legally required elements of a trust is . . . the beneficiary. The beneficiary—not the trust creator (who may be long gone) or the trustee—is the single most important person to the existence of a trust. No beneficiary, no trust. And yet, too often, when trusts are created or being administered, the beneficiaries are treated as afterthoughts or annoyances.

Recent Trends in Trust Law

In the United States, trust relationships are governed by state law. Depending on how a state's courts have ruled on the cases that have come before them, you can find sharply different interpretations of trust law in one state versus another. It further follows that some states have a more richly developed case law than others, depending on the volume and variety of cases heard by their courts.

While competing with each other for trust business, recent decades have seen states also attempt to make trust law more consistent from state to state. Founded in 1892, the National Conference of Commissioners on Uniform State Laws (NCCUSL) is a group of well-respected private lawyers, government lawyers, legislators, judges, and law professors. Members of the NCCUSL are appointed by their respective state governments. Their mission is to "research, draft and promote enactment of uniform state laws in areas of state law where uniformity is desirable and practical."[3]

Once NCCUSL has drafted a "uniform act,"—and such an act can cover areas of law well beyond estates and trusts—it's up to each state's legislature to decide whether to adopt the act. States have flexibility to adopt a uniform act in its entirety, adopt portions of the act, adopt a revised version of the act, or not adopt the act at all.

In 2000, NCCUSL proposed the *Uniform Trust Code (UTC)*. The UTC provides a model for codifying certain aspects of the law of trust relationships. To date, slightly more than half the states have adopted some version of the UTC. The UTC is but one of many statutes passed by state legislatures that affect trust relationships.

Despite the promotion and adoption of the UTC, as statutes affecting trusts have proliferated, there's been little coordination between and among jurisdictions. Today, codification of laws governing trust relationships varies from state to state in significant ways.

For example, states are sorting out into "trust-creator intent" jurisdictions and "beneficiary protective" jurisdictions. Traditionally, great deference is given to the intent of the trust creator. In some jurisdictions, this orientation toward enforcing the trust creator's intent is shifting toward a "sole-benefit-of-the-beneficiaries" principle. In these jurisdictions, it's easier for beneficiaries to modify a trust or to use the starker alternative of "decanting." As we discuss more fully in Chapter 17, to decant means to terminate a trust and move the assets to a new trust that has more favorable provisions.

A sampling of other differences among jurisdictions include

- The degree to which trust property is protected from creditors.
- The ease of suing a trustee.
- The length of time a trust can last.
- The ability to divide fiduciary duties among co-trustees. For example, one co-trustee may be the designated fiduciary for investments. Other co-trustees need not be concerned about investments, and would not be held liable if things go wrong.

The point of all this is that it's very important for trust creators to have conversations with their attorney to flesh out the trust creator's intent in detail (especially as it relates to the beneficiaries' welfare), and that "location, location, location" can make a difference.

A Closing Exercise

So much for trusts in general. If what you just read sounded overly theoretical, here's a lively exercise to prepare you for one or more conversations with your fellow trustscapers and/or legal counsel. (We purposely don't touch on the tax consequences of the language of your trust. Please reserve such questions for the session with your legal counsel.)

What we have in mind is a treasure hunt, using your trust agreement as the field for your hunting. (If many trusts impact your life, then choose one that plays or will play an especially large role.) When we say "lively" exercise, we aren't being sarcastic. True, much of your trust document will likely be boilerplate, that is, standard language to save taxes, administer the trust, and so on. Boilerplate tends to be legalese and boring. Still, don't skip over it.

So what is the treasure? We offer questions below to guide your hunting. These questions are not all-inclusive, but they do cover a lot of ground. The answers are your "treasures"—a few of which will indeed be hidden among the boilerplate.

Because the rules for this "hunt" are anything but rigid, feel free to add questions as you go. Happy hunting!

Basic Questions to Answer

- Who created the trust?
- What is its discernible purpose?
- When does the trust take effect?
- Who is the trustee(s)?
- What property is governed by the trust? (See the most recent statement prepared by the trustee for the current list of trust assets.)
- Who is entitled to receive distributions from the trust now? Are there beneficiaries who will receive distributions later?

Questions Regarding the Trustee

- If I have more than one trustee, are the duties divided among them?
- If the current trustee resigns or is removed, who is the successor?
- Can the beneficiary remove and replace the trustee?
- Sometimes, rather than naming a successor trustee directly, a process is described for doing so. If so, what is that process?

Question Regarding the Trust Property

- Are there special instructions for managing any of the trust property?

Questions Regarding Trust Distributions

- Are some distributions automatic (e.g., distribution of income)? Are some distributions scheduled (e.g., when a beneficiary reaches a certain age)?
- The trustee is often given discretion to make distributions. If so, for what purposes may the trustee make discretionary distributions?

Questions on the Trust Protector and Trust Committees

- Is a trust protector appointed?
- If so, what powers are granted to the trust protector? A trust protector often has the job of seeing that the trust's purposes are fulfilled.
- Are one or more trust committees created?
- If so, what are their purposes?

Questions on When the Trust Terminates

- When does my trust come to an end? When the beneficiary reaches a certain age? At someone's death?
- What happens to the trust assets when the trust terminates? Does the property go to someone outright? Does it get moved to some other trust?
- Does someone have a right to determine who receives the trust property? If so, how is that right exercised?

  Once you have collected your treasures from this hunt, ask:

- What surprised you?
- What delighted you?
- What confused you?

Next Steps

- What additional questions do you have?
- Who is the best person to answer your questions?

Congratulations—if you completed the hunt and answered most or even all of the questions we posed here, then you have become far more familiar with your trust than many trustscapers ever do. As one of our colleagues said to us, "If I could give one piece of advice to trustees and beneficiaries, it is, 'Read the trust.'" We would add only, "Re-read it too."

Notes

1. In succeeding chapters, the authors refer to the trust creator's "intent." When we do, we are not referring to the trust creator's express intent to create a trust. Rather, we use *intent* interchangeably with the trust creator's "motivation" or "purpose" for creating the trust.

2. Restatement Third Trusts §27, Comment on Subsection 2. The *Restatement of the Law Third, Trusts,* is published by the American Law Institute. The *Restatement* is compiled by a reporter, several associate reporters, and dozens of advisers and consultants who are leading attorneys, professors, and judges. The *Restatement* "draws both on court decisions and statutes, seeking a seamless statement of the best principles of American trust law . . ." (from the Foreword).

3. www.uniformlawcommission.com/Narrative.aspx?title=About%20the%20ULC.

Chapter 6

The Trustee

In Part One of this book, we introduced you to the "trust-scape" rather than just the trust. As you then saw in Chapter 5, a "trust" colloquially refers to a document that defines certain rights, duties, and relationships. The "trustscape" is the system that includes not only these rights, duties, and legal relationships, but also the interpersonal relationships among the human beings and institutions that possess these rights, duties, and relationships. For many families, their trustscape includes multiple trusts amid other legal entities.

In this chapter and Chapters 7 and 8, we want to take a closer look at some of these trees in the forest of the trustscape. We want to dwell on the roles that people or institutions occupy within it. As you read these three chapters, try to locate yourself within these roles and within this landscape. It may be that you find yourself in multiple positions. That is not at all unusual. The trustscape is a world in which you can be in more than one place at the same time.

The Trustee

The trustee is the one who is literally "entrusted" with the property held in trust. To use a term from one of our prior books, the trustee keeps alive the "cycle of the gift" initiated by the trust creator.

Within this overarching purpose, the trustee has several responsibilities and also several duties.

The main responsibilities of the trustee are threefold: administration of the trust, investment of the trust's assets, and the distribution of benefits to the beneficiary.

Administration encompasses accounting for the trust's assets—that is, keeping track of them—if necessary distinguishing the trust's income from the principal that generates that income, and filing the trust's tax returns and any other required disclosures or reports. Administration does not sound exciting—and indeed it is not exciting . . . until someone really needs a document or an accounting years down the road. Too often family members or their advisers no longer have copies. It then falls upon the shoulders of the well-prepared trustee to prove its administrative mettle.

For most trustees who are not professional investors, the *investment* responsibility involves selecting an investment adviser who understands the particular requirements for investing trust assets; establishing a process to identify and keep updated the trust's investment policy; tracking and benchmarking the trust's investment results; and (unless directed otherwise by the trust document itself) making sure that the trust's assets are held in a well-diversified portfolio that comports with modern portfolio theory, that is, which balances expected returns against expected risk and volatility, using an investment policy statement as a guide.

The *distributive* responsibility is, in our view, the most important and often the most overlooked of the trustee's three main responsibilities. Sometimes that responsibility extends only to distributing out the trust's income and leaving the principal untouched. Sometimes the trust document will direct the trust to make distributions of principal at specific ages of the beneficiary. Very often, however, the trustee will be granted "discretion" to distribute income and even principal for certain types of needs (e.g., "health, education, maintenance, and support") or *only* as the trustee sees fit. (The latter type of discretion is known as "absolute discretion.") In the cases of discretionary distributions, the trustee may establish a process to understand the true needs of the beneficiary, including the beneficiary's current financial situation, educational or work plans, and other personal details.

Governing all three of these responsibilities are certain duties. These duties are not a "wish list" of "nice to haves." Shaped by centuries of judicial decisions and legislation, they are "must haves" or "must do's" that can be enforced at law. When fully explained, the duties of a trustee can encompass many thick books. Here we will offer just a thumbnail sketch of three of the most important *duties*:

The duty to account: It seems relatively simple—if you are entrusted with something, you must be able to tell where you left it—but, of course, with financial instruments or even real property, this requirement can be tricky. Also, in many jurisdictions, this duty carries with it the requirement to send an annual accounting of the trust's performance to adult beneficiaries. This requirement can be tough to swallow for parents and trustees of beneficiaries who are legally adults but who may be harmed by knowing that they are beneficiaries of a trust.

The duty of care: A trust is not a safe and a trustee is not a guard, watching over the trust property with no purpose. The trust exists to benefit some beneficiary, and the trustee must take care to understand the beneficiary's true needs and act accordingly.

The duty of impartiality: Even though many trusts are established with a particular *primary* beneficiary in mind, almost all trusts have multiple beneficiaries or even classes of beneficiaries. For example, a trust may benefit first one child and then that child's own children. Or a trust may benefit a spouse and then, when that spouse is dead, a charity. The trustee has a duty to serve the interests of all the beneficiaries, impartially, not just the ones who are alive, most vocal, or most likeable.

These purposes, responsibilities, and duties help shape the trustee's *function*. As far as the trustee's *form*, it can take a number of shapes.

An individual ("natural") person can serve as trustee. That person may be a professional or a layman. The most common professionals to serve as trustees are lawyers, accountants, or financial advisers. Sometimes the attorney who drafted the trust document will be named as trustee. Sometimes a trust creator will want the chief financial officer of his company or a longtime corporate attorney to serve as an *individual trustee*.

Laymen trustees may include the spouse of the trust creator, or his or her siblings, children, cousins, partners, or best friend. Again, as the title implies, the main criterion for a trustee is not necessarily any expertise but rather a moral one: it is someone that the trust creator deeply trusts to uphold his or her wishes with regard to the trust.

But individual people are not the only trustees. Some corporations or companies make it their business to serve as trustees. In such cases, the trustee is referred to as an *institutional trustee*. An institutional trustee employs trust officers and others to serve its trust clients. It almost always has a trust review committee to accept client trusts and a distribution committee to decide on discretionary distribution requests. Even though human beings staff these committees, the company itself is the trustee.

It will make sure to keep its clients' trust assets separate from its own. That way, even if the business fails, trust clients should be able to retrieve their assets without loss.

Choices

Just as painters have choices in composing a landscape, trust creators and sometimes beneficiaries also have choices in assembling the trustscape. The most significant is likely the choice of trustee. This is for many people a very difficult choice, as it involves many factors and often requires making guesses at what will be required to serve the good of beneficiaries who are still young children or maybe not even born.

In thinking through the choice of individual versus institutional trustees, many people find it helpful to compare the pros and cons of each. The table below is a high-level summary of some possible pros and cons. Some may apply to some trustees and not others. We encourage you to add your own thoughts to this list:

The distinctions offered in this table are, of course, general and may not capture well the practices of specific individual or institutional trustees. For example, there is a growing movement among some institutional trustees to incorporate into their practices increased personal attention to the individual beneficiaries of the families they serve, thereby combining some of the best qualities of an individual trustee with the strengths of an institutional trustee. Also, we have not attempted to address here the pros and cons of private trust companies (PTCs), which are becoming more popular among ultra-high-net-worth families. For more on PTCs, please see Appendix 4.

The most desirable choice is always to have one's cake and eat it, too. Some families make this choice by splitting up the responsibilities of the trustee among several different types of trustees. For example, they may ask an institutional trustee to

Category	Individual Trustees		Institutional Trustees	
	Pros	Cons	Pros	Cons
Connection	Personal: a human being who is accessible to you.	Perhaps too close: having a family member or friend serve as trustee may change your relationship.	Professional representatives usually called trust officers or relationship managers.	A trust officer who you have gotten to know may leave or be replaced. You will have to start anew with someone else. It may be hard to connect with a decision-maker.
Knowledge	Probably knows who you are and how your family works.	Depending on his or her background, may have little or no expertise in law, investing, or other topics important to trust administration.	Trust officers typically have lots of expertise in the legal, financial, and administrative aspects of trusts.	A trust officer may serve many clients and may not know much about you or your family.
Process	You know who makes the decisions and can ask him or her to explain those decisions.	Professional individual trustees usually are formal in their processes. Laymen trustees, such as family members, may not be so formal, which can lead to confusion.	Institutional trustees tend to be very formal in their processes. Decisions are often strongly influenced by "risk management" considerations.	Their processes can sometimes feel laborious, and it can be hard to identify who, if anyone, is the decision-maker in a given situation.
Liability	Individual trustees take on personal liability. If you have a problem, you know where they live.	If you have a problem, are you going to sue your uncle or your sister? Suing a well-prepared lawyer or accountant is also not an attractive prospect.	Institutional trustees carry plenty of insurance and usually have the assets to make whole a beneficiary harmed by poor trust administration.	Institutional trustees are very able to defend themselves in cases alleging mismanagement.
Cost	An individual trustee may cost little or nothing, especially if it's a friend or family member.	You may get what you pay for.	Institutional trustees often have clear fee schedules for their work as trustees.	A trustee fee can add a quarter or half a percent to already existing investment management fees. These fees add up quickly.

serve as trustee solely for the administrative function or for both the administrative and investment function, while an individual trustee—someone who knows the family and the beneficiaries— serves as trustee solely for distributive decisions. We offer an innovative model arrangement of trustee duties in Part Four of this book.

This "delegation" of functions (or even more strongly, the "direction" of a trustee to hand over some of its functions to, say, a specific investment adviser) is not possible in every jurisdiction or for every trust. You will have to consult with your legal counsel to see what would work for you. Delegation and direction have the downside of adding complexity to an already complicated topic. Complexity may in turn bring with it confusion, conflict, and costs. Nevertheless, the gains of identifying specialized trustees and other advisers to serve these different functions can be great.

One more point is important to consider regarding the choice of trustee or co-trustees. Conflicts of interest are rife in trustscapes. For example, sometimes the attorney who drafts the trust document also includes him- or herself as trustee: is it likely that this family adviser will sue him- or herself for inadequate drafting or poor trust management? Similarly, an institutional trustee may offer great administrative services but lackluster investment management, and yet not want to give up the latter activity because it is where it can charge the greatest fees.

There is no magical solution to these conflicts. The key is to acknowledge the conflicts that exist, document them, make sure all parties (the trust creator, the trustees, the trust protector, and the adult beneficiaries) are aware of them, and if necessary, develop processes for managing the conflicts.

This awareness of conflicts of interest points to the importance of the *character* of the people involved in the trustee function. We have shared here some things to consider regarding the *type* of trustee. Clearly, the choice of *who* to serve as trustee—whether that "who" is an individual trustee or the representative of an institutional trustee—is just as important or even more important. When weighing this choice, think back to the Introduction, to the discussion of the principles underlying trusteeship. Ask yourself: does the proposed trustee or trust officer see this work as a noble profession, which starts with doing no harm? Does he or she understand fidelity and regency? Has he or she shown discretion? Has he or she demonstrated courage and the ability to encourage others? These qualities are intangible but also of incalculable importance.

For other qualities to look for or questions to ask when selecting an individual trustee (or evaluating a trust officer of an institutional trustee), please see our discussion of what to consider if someone asks you to serve as trustee, in Chapter 9.

We recognize that finding a trustee who has all of these qualities may be impossible. And if you are fortunate to find such a person, he or she may decline to serve as trustee. In Part Four, we describe how a trustscape may nevertheless be designed to include all of these qualities by creatively and thoughtfully allocating functions among other trustscapers in addition to the trustee.

Chapter 7

Beneficiaries and Trust Creators

Several years ago, two of us (Jay Hughes and Keith Whitaker, along with our partner, Dr. Susan Massenzio) wrote *The Cycle of the Gift*, a book focused on how parents and grandparents can give wisely to their children and grandchildren. As we were writing that book, we came to a realization: while there were many books written to parents about the impact of monetary gifts to their children, there were very few if any books written to adult children—the recipients of these gifts—and even fewer written from the perspective of these recipients. This gap in publishing, we saw, reflected an even deeper problem: the point of view of the recipient, and the experience of receiving, is persistently ignored.

Everyone loves a giver. But few people, if any, appear to want to think about much less talk about recipients.

Slighting recipients would remain an abstract problem, perhaps even a nonproblem, if it were not for one basic fact: givers who think only about themselves and not at all about their recipients tend to make very bad gifts. We do not mean "bad" in a moral sense, though overlooking the recipient's experience of receiving can lead to terrible results, such as dependency and entitlement. We mean even more basically, "ineffective" or "unproductive."

As the Roman philosopher Seneca said, "The manner in which a gift is given determines the manner in which it is received." A gift given out of a desire for control will likely lead to either passivity or resistance. A gift given out of absent-mindedness will inspire a similar lack of care. A gift that was really not intended to be given but merely to save taxes will likely not be seen as a gift but rather as a lucky strike, an undeserved boon. A gift given grudgingly will hardly be received thankfully.

In our many years of practice and in the years since we wrote *Cycle of the Gift*, we have seen all these different variations on giving and receiving and many more. These observations caused us to distinguish between "transfers" and "gifts with spirit." Transfers are the mere movement of money from one person's balance sheet to another's. Transfers may be grudging or absent-minded or poorly thought out or even highly sophisticated and controlling, with all sorts of "strings attached." What they are not are true gifts with spirit. Gifts with spirit, in contrast, are made freely and received freely. They have clear purpose and intention. They are made based on an understanding of who the recipient is and how to help that person integrate the gift into his or her life. Because they are made well, they are more likely to be received well.

In *Cycle of the Gift*, we used an image to capture the power and complexity of gifts, the image of a "meteor" that speeds from

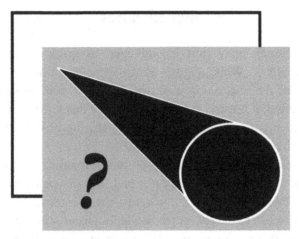

Figure 7.1 What's in Your Meteor?

the giver to the recipient (see Figure 7.1). Gifts can be like meteors in that they often appear out of nowhere and suddenly crash into the recipient's "atmosphere," even knocking the recipient off his or her life's path. Also, every gift contains within it some sort of spirit or message. As we have mentioned, that message may be one of control or even contempt. It may be a spirit of freedom, encouragement, and love. For trust creators we ask, "What is in your meteor?" For beneficiaries, we ask, "What has your meteor brought into your world?"

Because giving and receiving are so closely tied together, we decided here to present in one chapter thoughts on the *roles* of trust creator and beneficiary. Again, most of the time these roles are treated in isolation (if they are treated at all). In contrast, we believe that to be a great trust creator you must pay attention to and understand what it takes to be a great beneficiary. And, likewise, we believe that to be a great beneficiary you must attend to and understand what it takes to be a great trust creator. Because they are so often given short shrift, we will begin here with beneficiaries.

Beneficiaries

Many readers may find it odd even to speak about "great beneficiaries." What is great about receiving money you did not earn? At best, doing so is usually seen as something lucky. More often, it is seen as something slightly shameful. It is hard to imagine anyone announcing to others that he or she is a "great beneficiary."

These judgments reflect a common prejudice: that earning money is good and receiving it is bad. But this belief overlooks that receiving money *well* is not a passive, easy activity. Sure, it takes no effort to have your trustee deposit money into your bank account. But it takes a great deal of effort to spend that money wisely and to truly integrate it into your life, to make sure that the "meteor" does not knock you off course but rather brings new resources to your world. Most simply, what we advocate is that beneficiaries become *active recipients*.

Most people structure their lives around making money. There are many careers to choose among in order to pursue that goal. There are many paths within those careers, which are well marked out. Every discipline or job has its own "ladder" to climb. Most people climbing those ladders think little or not at all about whether they are doing the "right" thing.

What, then, about the life that does not have to aim at making money? Where are the guideposts or road maps for someone for whom the question is not, "How do I make a living?" but rather, "Given that I have money, how do I live well?" Where are the prerequisites, qualifications, educational paths, or the corporate "ladder" to climb? There are none. With such a dearth of directions, this job—to integrate unearned money into a good life—starts to look much harder than the typical career path. And yet beneficiaries must make this effort at the very same time that most of the authorities in their lives tell them that they have it easy. Doing it well takes active effort.

Becoming a great beneficiary means facing the core question of life: How can I live well? If someone faces that question effectively, then he or she certainly deserves the adjective *great*.

How can a beneficiary begin to meet that challenge? After we wrote *Cycle of the Gift*, we took up this question in a second volume, *The Voice of the Rising Generation*, which was addressed specifically to 20-, 30-, and 40-somethings in families with wealth. We will encapsulate here some of the main messages from that book, while encouraging readers to turn there for more depth:

- First, ask yourself, "What are my dreams?" What are the activities you feel best in? When do you "flow"? Spend some time and don't judge your answers. They will, over time, give direction to the rest of your life.[1]

- Then, ask yourself what are your strengths and what are the internal hurdles you have to jump over in order to pursue your dreams? More specifically, what beliefs—about yourself, your family, the world—do you feel support you and what beliefs hold you back? How can you strengthen the former set of beliefs and how can you begin to change the latter?

- When have you worked—for someone else's company or enterprise or benefit? Have you ever been an apprentice to a specific discipline or field? What can you learn from those experiences? If you don't have such experiences, where can you turn to find them?

- When you think about the important relationships in your life, which ones affirm your strengths? Which friends or family members share your dreams? Do you have relationships with people who are positive and forward focused? Do you have relationships with people who challenge you to be the best you can be? If not, where can you look to cultivate such relationships?

- Do you feel able to advocate for yourself and your dreams to your parents or trustees? Do you even feel you understand the trusts or other structures that impact your life financially and beyond? If not, what are steps you can take to increase your understanding or to develop your skills?

These are large questions, and naturally they take us far beyond the confines of the trustscape and the relationship between a beneficiary and his or her trustees. But it is possible to adapt the spirit of these questions to that relationship as well. Our co-author Jay Hughes did so in his first book *Family Wealth*, and we have reproduced his list of the roles and *responsibilities* of beneficiaries. Again, many people may find it strange to think that a beneficiary—a recipient—has any role or responsibilities. But that view ignores the real work involved in receiving well. Indeed, these are duties that you owe not to others but rather to yourself.

There is one more step that we encourage beneficiaries to take in order to become active recipients. It involves gratitude.

There has been a great deal of research in recent years showing the beneficial effects of gratitude on people's lives.[2] Gratitude helps move our attention away from negative and towards positive emotions; we focus on what we have rather than what we don't have. Even small instances of gratitude—saying, "Thank you," to a stranger who holds the door for you out or calling up a relative to say how glad you are to have him or her in your life—can have a lasting impact. It is no exaggeration to say that gratitude may be one of the keys to happiness.

And yet, for all that beneficiaries receive, gratitude is sometimes hard. That may be because the trust creator is long gone—and perhaps never even knew the beneficiary he or she has benefited. It may be because the source of wealth involved products or processes that conflict with the beneficiary's values. It can be that the beneficiary feels ashamed to receive money he or she did not earn.

ROLES AND RESPONSIBILITIES OF BENEFICIARIES

Each beneficiary has an obligation to educate himself or herself about the duties of a beneficiary, as well as the duties of the family trustees. Here are specific responsibilities of beneficiaries:

- To gain a clear comprehension of each trust in which the beneficiary has an interest and a specific understanding of the mission statement for each trust as prepared by the trustees
- To educate himself or herself about all trustee responsibilities
- To understand the trustee's responsibility to maintain the purchasing power of the trust's capital while maintaining a reasonable distribution rate for the income beneficiaries
- To have a general understanding of modern portfolio theory and the formation and process of asset allocation
- To recognize and look for proof that each trustee represents all beneficiaries
- To meet with each trustee once each year to discuss his or her personal financial circumstances and personal goals and to advise the trustee of his or her assessment of the trustee's performance of the trustee roles and responsibilities to the trust, to the beneficiary, and to family governance
- To become knowledgeable about the functions and importance of each element of the family's trust governance structure
- To attend the annual family business meeting and to accept responsible roles within the family governance structure, based on his or her qualifications for such roles
- To develop a general capacity to understand fiduciary accounting
- To demonstrate a willingness to participate in educational sessions and to become financially literate (through family seminars and family-funded educational programs)
- To know how and in what amount trustees and other professionals are compensated and to obtain a general understanding of the budgets for the trust and investment entities in which the trust will be invested

It can also be hard to express gratitude when the trust creator's wishes conflict with the beneficiary's own dreams. For example, a woman we once met was the beneficiary of trust set up by her grandfather, who said that the primary purpose for the trust was to pay for her wedding or a down-payment on a house. She did not plan to marry, and she was also not planning to buy a house anytime soon. But she had returned to school and was trying to handle courses and hold down a full-time job. What she really needed was a car, to get from classes, to work, and back. Her trustee and she found a way to make a distribution to help her buy the car. As grateful as she was, however, she could not express her gratitude directly to her grandfather; she felt that he just would not understand.

We mention these difficulties because the fact is that, without some expression of gratitude, a gift remains incomplete, and an incomplete gift lacks spirit. It cannot become truly integrated into the recipient's life. It remains external, even a burden. This is one of the reasons that in some countries, France, for example, recipients *must* acknowledge a gift for it to become complete.

With this moral reality in mind, then, we recommend that beneficiaries try out some sort of gratitude exercise with regard to their trust. Perhaps it is speaking directly to the trust creator and explaining what sorts of positive impact the trust has had on your life. If the trust creator is no long alive, perhaps it means writing a letter to him or her that you keep in your files. Or you could send this letter to the current trustee. If your relationship with the trust creator or trustee has been challenging, then maybe the expression becomes simply reflecting on what you have learned from your experience as a beneficiary.

This is not an exercise that needs to be repeated on a daily or weekly basis. But it makes sense to practice it once or twice a year. You may be surprised how your expressions of gratitude change over the years as your trust or trusts play different roles in your changing life. Truly, finding some authentic expression of gratitude is key to becoming an active recipient.

Trust Creators

What are the corresponding role and responsibilities of a trust creator? Again, even speaking about the trust creator's responsibilities may sound strange. What responsibilities does someone have in giving away his or her own money? Isn't it a free gift, to be made as the giver sees fit?

There is no doubt that freedom is a key component of giving. But freedom and responsibility are not at odds. Indeed, most parents say to their children, "With freedom comes responsibility." The two are inseparable. For example, you don't get the keys to the car until you can prove that you can drive it responsibly, that is, without posing a danger to yourself and others. Responsibility gives shape to the exercise of true freedom.

Of course, there are no car keys for a new trust; nor is there a driver's license exam. Only the individual trust creator can decide whether he or she is ready to make a responsible gift, a gift with spirit, in the form of a trust. Our experience is that most of us are not ready, even when we think we are. Taking this step may take a great deal of time and deliberation. It is not something to hurry along because of perceived deadlines due to changing tax laws or the like. Though it may be heresy to some accountants and tax attorneys, we say it is better to pay some tax today than to put the entire capital of the gift at risk as it becomes a destructive meteor for generations to come. Put most simply, we encourage trust creators to be *active givers*.

How, then, can a wise trust creator give actively and responsibly? To begin, one must acknowledge the importance of acting with intention or, as our friend and colleague John A. Warnick puts it, of acting "purposefully." Unlike in the case of the beneficiaries, a trust creator's duties are not to him- or herself, primarily, but to others, to the beneficiaries. Fulfilling those duties to others requires thought and care. It requires purposefulness.

A first step in purposeful giving is to ask yourself, "Am I truly a trust creator?" Most people are actually trust *signers*. That is, they sign a trust document drafted by an attorney, a document largely if not wholly composed of "boilerplate." There is nothing creative about it. Indeed, if you find yourself plowing through reams of documents in one sitting, you may not even be a trust signer: you may be more of a trust stamper!

To act creatively requires first understanding where you are coming from in this work. We encourage trust creators to ask themselves these additional questions:

- What is an example of a gift that you have made that *enhanced* your life and the life of your recipient? It may have been a big gift; it may have been small. The size is not the issue but rather the spirit.
- What is an example of a gift that you made or received that did *not* enhance the lives of the giver and of the recipient? Interestingly, most people find it easier to think of these negative, failed gifts than examples of positive, successful ones. This goes to show how hard it is to give well.
- What challenges are you facing now in your giving and how do you plan to address those challenges?

Our past experiences with giving always affect our present or future attempts to give well. If we do not acknowledge those experiences, we lose the benefit of learning from them, and we open ourselves to being controlled, unconsciously, by their effects. That is the very opposite of acting purposefully.

Some additional questions may help you as a trust creator gain even greater clarity about yourself, as a giver, in preparation for making a gift with spirit:

- Where are you in your life? That is, where are you in your own stage of development? Making a gift at age 40 is very different from making a gift at age 80. Our hopes and aspirations change as we go through the stages of our life. These hopes and aspirations will naturally affect our expectations of our gifts.
- What do you want to achieve? This question refers more to the desired outcome of the gift than to its purpose or

intention. A gift's purpose may be to enhance the life of the beneficiary. One of its outcomes may be to restrict funds in the case that the beneficiary shows signs of addiction. Sometimes the toughest conversations among givers and recipients concern the seeming disparity between intentions and outcomes. People often see only today's outcome and miss the enduring intention.

- Does the gift reflect your values? This is a fundamental question for every giver. All of us have values, deeply held beliefs, which govern our choices and our feelings. Sometimes we do not acknowledge those values clearly enough, and as a result we become angry when we see a gift we have made being used in ways that offend those values. In other cases givers make adherence to their values a condition for receiving a gift, sparking resentment or resistance in the recipient. What your values are and to what degree you want them to govern the manner of your giving are questions only you can answer—but answering them before you give is crucial to giving well.
- Would this gift bring you joy? This is a question that requires some imagination to answer. Imagine that you have made the gift in trust and that it is now several decades later. The trust has played a role in the life of the beneficiary. What does its impact look like? What choices has it made possible? In what ways may it have held the beneficiary back? Does this vision bring you joy in your heart or pain? If the latter, then it may be important to rethink the trust.

Next, as a trust creator, ask yourself whether the gift in trust that you are contemplating or have made is a gift with spirit. That is,

- Does it have a clear intention or purpose?
- Is it focused on enhancing the lives of the beneficiaries?
- Has that purpose been clearly communicated to the beneficiaries?

In many cases, trust creators do have clear, positive purposes for their gifts, but when it comes to that third question, they balk: "How can I tell the beneficiaries about the trust? I may disincentivize them!" This concern is a very real one. While we encourage clear communication, it is also the case that communicating too soon may serve as that "meteor" that knocks a beneficiary off his or her life's path. Only you can tell whether that would be the case at this moment in time. If it seems possible that it would knock the recipient off course, then do not communicate the gift. But recognize at the same time that the gift is not truly complete—it remains a transfer—until the communication takes place. Focus, then, on how to help the beneficiary move to a place where such communication will be possible. And if it seems as though such a time will never come, then perhaps it would be wiser not to make the gift at all.

Just as it is crucial for a trust creator to understand him- or herself in order to give well, so too it is crucial to understand the intended beneficiary. No gift can be made well to someone you don't know or don't try to understand: any positive outcome in such cases is mere luck. To this end, ask yourself these questions about the intended recipient:

- Where is the recipient in his or her life? That is, what stage of development? Making a gift to a teenager is naturally much different than setting up a trust for someone in middle age.
- What is the recipient's character? Can you trust him or her? Does the recipient habitually make good choices or bad ones? These may be questions that are painful to face, but they must be faced if you are to make an honest appraisal of the recipient's ability to receive well.
- What is the recipient's temperament? Temperament is different than character: it is more the way that the recipient is in the world: slow versus hasty, gentle versus angry. Temperament

can be annoying, but it does not rise to being offensive the way bad character does.

- What money skills and knowledge does the recipient possess? It is not necessary for a great recipient to have an MBA. But, as described earlier, some basic understanding is a responsibility of a great beneficiary. If the recipient does not have such knowledge and skills, how can you or the trustee help him or her develop them?

- How resilient is the beneficiary? This is a core question, since resilience affects the beneficiary's ability to integrate the "meteor" of the trust into his or her life. Resilience is the ability to "bounce back" from challenges. It is partly genetic and partly learned. It can be developed through work, apprenticeship, sports, and other demanding activities. If the recipient has not displayed resilience, how can you or the trustee help him or her increase resilience?

At this point you may be getting close to finalizing your trust and making the gift. If you have done so based on a true understanding of yourself and your recipient, then bravo: you are ahead of most trust creators. Just as some knowledge of the trust itself is imperative in the case of a beneficiary, it is also true—and maybe even more so—in the case of the trust creator. To that end, among the responsibilities of trust creators we include these points:

- To gain a clear comprehension of the trust agreement.
- To educate yourself about the responsibilities of the trustees and (if applicable) trust protectors.
- To understand the trustee's duty to balance the interests of present beneficiaries and remainder or contingent beneficiaries.
- To understand, in a basic sense, modern portfolio theory and its application to trust asset allocation.

- To look for proof that each trustee represents all beneficiaries.
- To meet with the trustees at least once a year to assess the trustee's performance, especially with a view toward the development of beneficiaries.

We share these responsibilities because they are, in a way, both broader and narrower than the approach that many trust creators take to their trusts. Many trust creators see the trusts they establish as "my money." As a result, they may contact trustees frequently, demanding better investment performance, and bristling at trustees' comments that trusts cannot be managed the same as personal funds. These responsibilities should help trust creators see that, because trust funds are not personal funds, their management is different and, indeed, the main question is not, "What return are the trust's investments making?" but rather, "What impact is the trust having in the life of the beneficiary?"

Finally, we come back to the topic of communication. As mentioned earlier, a gift is not complete—it remains a transfer— so long as it is not communicated. When your recipients are independent adults, we recommend a three-step process for making this communication (we discuss this three-step process at more length in Chapter 16):

- First, clarify what you want to communicate, and then discuss this with your spouse or partner. Together, plan the communication with your children or other recipients, whether that will be one on one or all together. It is usually less stressful and more manageable to communicate one on one, though parents must be mindful that children speak with each other, so their communication should be consistent.
- Second, hold the conversation with your adult child. Use it as an opportunity to "seek to understand." Share what you have decided to share, and then listen. See what questions your child has. See how he or she reacts. Remind your would-be recipient that to discuss the topic is not to decide the matter.

You retain the prerogative to change your mind as you finalize your plans. But you would like his or her input. Sometimes children have very helpful thoughts, especially when it comes to structuring trusts for their own children, your grandchildren. Listen to their thoughts and make notes.

• Third, reflect on what you learned in the conversations with your adult children. Decide with your spouse or partner if there are changes that you want to make to your plans. If there are changes, make sure to communicate those changes to your children. Loop back to them in any event to let them know your planning is complete and that you appreciate their involvement in it.

Such a process is easier to describe than to do. But we have seen many couples go through it in this step-by-step way and come out the other end feeling good about the results. It takes time and it takes honest, sometimes difficult conversations with your spouse and children. But proceeding methodically greatly decreases the likelihood that there will be difficult conversations or even conflict after you are gone.

But what about when you do not have independent, adult beneficiaries with whom to communicate in this reasonable fashion? What if your recipients are children or even unborn? What if they are disabled by addictions?

In the case of addiction, we recommend that trust creators carefully consider the recommendations offered by Bill Messinger in Chapter 15, which focuses on this difficult area.

In the case of minor or unborn recipients, you must simply accept that *you are not making a truly completed gift:* you are making a transfer and relying on the trustee to complete the gift. This is a crucial point to recognize. In such cases, you must rely on the trustee to infuse the gift with spirit. To do so, the trustee will have to rely on your guidance and direction, sometimes in the form of written letters of wishes or the "Preamble" to your trust as described in Chapter 10. You will also need to give the trustee the discretion to shape the spirit of the eventual gift to the character and qualities of the future recipients.

Again, no one can give well to someone he does not even know. This inability points to a last consideration in such cases: you must trust your trustee. The choice of trustee and design of the trustscape become highly important when you are making a transfer to minor or unborn recipients, for it is the trustee (perhaps supported by the Distribution Committee that we describe in Chapter 20 and Appendix 3) who will turn that transfer into a true gift with spirit. Who can serve well in such a role? As a starting point, reconsider the principles that we describe in the Introduction, particularly an understanding of the principle of regency.

We want to end with one more question, at least for people who are considering becoming trust creators: what do you want to name your trust? This may seem like a minor matter. In fact, it usually gets handled in a cursory fashion, as documents are flying about, being prepared for signing. As a result, most trusts end up with cumbersome names, composed of the name of the giver, a date, and perhaps some legalese describing the type of trust. For example, "The John Doe 2015 Grantor Retained Annuity Trust."

But if you think ahead a few years, what is it that your beneficiaries are going to see of this trust? They will get a copy of the trust agreement, but unless they read the first part of this chapter, they may pay little attention to that. However, at some point in their adult lives, they will start receiving monthly or quarterly statements from whomever's managing the trust assets. And at the top of those statements will be the name of the trust. Do you want that name to appear to them to be gibberish? Do you want to remind them of a date that probably does not mean anything to them? As worthy as you are, do you want the name to be all about you?

Instead, are there other words, perhaps expressing values, that you would prefer to pass before your beneficiaries' eyes each time they open a trust statement? What are those words? Perhaps some of them would make a fine name for a trust. Coming up with a meaningful trust name is a small but powerful step in active giving.

Notes

1. For more on flow and dreams, see the classic work by Mihaly Czikszentmihalyi, *Flow: The Psychology of Optimal Experience* (New York: Harper, 2000).

2. See, for example, Martin Seligman, *Authentic Happiness* (New York: Free Press, 2002), Chapter Five, and many other books thereafter.

Chapter 8

The Trust Protector and the Trust Adviser

People often imagine a trust to be something like a safe, with the trustee keeping watch over it. The beneficiary may even be considered a safecracker, looking for an opening and a way to get the goods.

We disputed this version of the trustee in the prior two chapters. If a trust is nothing but a safe, then it is not a trust: a trust requires someone, a beneficiary, for whom it does some good. The trustee is not a Brinks guard. He or she or it must play some distributive role. Indeed, that role is part of the trustee's highest purpose.

Nonetheless, the "guardian" version of the trustee is a powerful one. And it leads naturally to a question, first posed by the Roman poet Juvenal two millennia ago: *Quis custodiet ipsos custodes*? "Who shall guard the guardians themselves?"

Trust Advisers

The concern is a common one. If you are entrusting a bank, or an attorney, or a good friend with assets for the benefit of someone you care about, how can you be sure that the trustee will manage and distribute those assets as you wish? If the trustee is an individual, no doubt you have examined his or her character and find it trustworthy. If that individual is a professional, you also probably rely on his or her professional identity and ethics. And if the trustee is a company, you likely rely on its well-developed processes and procedures, as well as its concerns for its corporate reputation and fear of litigation.

Still, none of these safeguards are foolproof. Even people of good character can disagree. Professional ethics, procedures, reputation, and litigation cannot ensure unanimity with a trust creator's wishes.

As a result, sometimes the trustscape includes an additional character or set of characters known as trust advisers. Trust advisers are distinct from the attorneys or accountants who advise a family about the creation or modification of a trust—though these same professionals may also serve in the role of "trust adviser."

This role was developed to watch over the watchers, to guard the guardians. Typically it is written into the trust agreement, with some statement of the powers and responsibilities of the trust adviser, along with a description of how (or if) the trust adviser can select his, her, or its successor.

Common functions of the trust adviser include:

- Reviewing investment management decisions.
- Receiving and reviewing the trustee's accountings.
- Reviewing distributive decisions.

- Providing, when requested, insights to the trustee regarding the trust creator's wishes or hopes for the trust.
- Serving as a conduit between the trustee and beneficiaries, advising the trustee as to the true needs of beneficiaries.

In many of these ways, the trust adviser may serve as a sort of proxy for the trust creator him- or herself, a "stand-in" for a person who has passed away or who cannot, for legal reasons, attempt to influence the trustee. For this reason, a trust adviser is often a younger associate of the trust creator, someone who is deeply trusted and whom the trust creator may even look upon as a sort of "second self."

Very importantly, because the trust adviser does not have the power to make decisions for the trustee, the trust adviser is not a fiduciary. That means that the trust adviser is not required to act solely in the best interests of the beneficiaries of the trust. Also, the trust adviser is not subject to the liability of a trustee, along with the reputational and economic risks that such liability brings. The absence of fiduciary liability sometimes makes a trust adviser role more attractive to a family or business confidant with his or her own personal wealth to be concerned about.

Trust Protectors

Out of the role of trust adviser has grown an additional guardian, the trust protector. Trust protectors originally were developed to exercise specific administrative or tax functions for offshore trusts. But in the past two decades, they have become more common in domestic circumstances as well.

Some jurisdictions have also created legislation defining the trust protector role (e.g., the Uniform Trust Code includes trust protectors) and determining whether a trust protector does—or does not—have fiduciary duties similar to those of a trustee. Naturally, that determination is a significant factor in the minds of anyone considering whether to accept appointment as a trust protector. You should consult your trust counsel regarding the use of a trust protector in your jurisdiction.

Ideally, from the standpoint of a potential trust protector, the role is defined in such a way as to try to avoid fiduciary duties. Nevertheless, many trust protectors still manage to have wide-ranging powers. In this chapter we will review these broad powers. As this guide progresses, and particularly in Part 4, we will argue for a more narrow and focused application of the trust protector.

Starting with the broad range, some of the trust protector's powers may include:

- Removing or appointing trustees.
- Modifying the trust for tax purposes.
- Modifying beneficiaries' interests.
- Modifying powers of appointment.
- Changing the applicable law governing the trust.
- Terminating the trust.

A trust protector cannot benefit from the trust. But absent this restriction, and absent any acts of "bad faith" by the trust protector, his or her or its powers can be remarkably broad.

Of course, such broad powers raise the question, "Who shall guard the guardians?," to yet another level. As a result, some trusts specify that the trust protector shall spring into action only on certain conditions.

For example, as we discuss in more detail in Chapter 21, a trust protector may take a "judicial" role, as an "elder" within the family system. What this role entails looks something like this: A trust may specify that the trustee has absolute discretion to make distributions to the beneficiary in order to further that beneficiary's flourishing in life. It takes an enlightened trustee to exercise such discretion well. The trustee will need to take the time to get to know the beneficiary, his or her true needs, and the best ways to support and foster the beneficiary's growth and development. As the beneficiary grows and develops, he or she may take a different view of those needs than the trustee. This can lead to conflict over a distribution. In such a case, either party could ask the trust protector to spring into action to review the question and, in a mediator role, help resolve the conflict. Such mediation does not require that the trust protector decide the issue or approve (or deny) the distribution. Rather, as an elder, the trust protector would listen to both sides, reflect on the circumstances, and propose solutions for the two parties to consider. If matters remain at an impasse, then and only then could the trust protector be authorized to take more direct interventions, such as by removing the trustee and appointing another in his, her, or its place.

We have seen trust protectors act in such a judicial function with great success. One of the benefits of defining the trust protector's role in this way is that it preserves the integrity of the primacy of the relationship between the trustee and the beneficiary: neither is inclined to look to the trust protector as the true "power behind the throne." The trust protector's main function is to mediate, not decide. And that power arises only at the request of one or another of the parties. At the same time, the trust protector has the "teeth," if all else fails to resolve a serious impasse.

Choices

Given the sometimes broad and significant powers of a trust adviser or trust protector, the choice of an individual or company to fill such a role is a serious one. As mentioned, trust creators often look to someone like themselves to fill the role of trust adviser or trust protector: almost a "second self" to keep watch over an institutional or professional trustee and the beneficiaries.

This approach is natural, but it has its downside. A trust adviser or trust protector whom the trust creator selects because that person looks "just like me" will immediately be seen as such by the trustee and the beneficiaries. The result is that the trust adviser or trust protector will be branded as "Dad's" (or Mom's) "guy." For a professional or institutional trustee, such a choice may lead to conflict over the trust's investment strategy. Professional or institutional trustees often invest trust funds in ways that comport with their professional judgment but that are not as aggressive or risky as desired by the (nonprofessional) trust creator or his or her deputies. Choosing a trust adviser or protector who would invest "just like me" could set up years of conflict with a more judicious professional or institutional trustee.

For beneficiaries, the choice of such a trust adviser or protector can lead to years of conflict with a father or mother substitute. Making the trust adviser or protector serve *in loco parentis* could mean relegating adult beneficiaries to the *locus peurorum*—the place of perpetual children. There is no better way to raise trust fund babies than to treat adults as babies.

Especially in the case of a trust protector, it is tempting to choose someone whom you think would make a great trustee but who is unwilling to serve in the role of trustee because of fiduciary liability—and then give that trust protector every power possible. This happens frequently with trusted attorneys whose law-firms or malpractice insurance provider no longer allow them to serve as individual trustees. But, as mentioned above, making such a choice can set up a bitter conflict between the actual trustee and this "shadow" trustee.

For all these reasons, enlightened trust creators often resist the temptation to appoint a trust adviser or protector who looks just like them or who serves to do their bidding. Instead, they may look to an individual or company that excels in navigating the complex relationships formed among trustees, beneficiaries, trust creators, and trust advisers or protectors. (They may also ask adult beneficiaries to share their input and to interview prospective protectors.) This "systems sense" is perhaps the main criterion necessary in a good trust adviser or protector. From this systems sense follows attention to communication and to the need to share information in order to foster shared purpose and effective decision making.

Finally, a wise trust adviser or protector knows how to preserve the greatest asset that he or she or it has: the luxury to take the long view. Unlike a trustee, who is pressed by circumstances to attend to the day-to-day management of the trust as well as the here-and-now good of the beneficiary, the trust adviser or protector can attend to the role that the trust will play in the entire family's life for the next decade or even the next century. This long-term view is a great asset to build into any trustscape. Again, we will come back to the role of trust protector in Part 4, with ideas on how a well-structured trust protector function can play an important role in a whole new version of the trustscape.

Part Three

BUILDING GREAT RELATIONSHIPS

Chapter 9

Considerations Prior to Accepting Appointment as Trustee

At this point you should have a good sense of what is meant by a trustscape and who the main players are within that environment. But unlike a landscape or portrait painting, the trustscape and its denizens are alive. It is now time to put them into motion. The chapters in this part focus on the practice of building great relationships within the trustscape. We invite you always to keep your own situation in mind as you read so that you can consider how to apply these practices to your trustscape. But to help you get started, we will begin with another story.

Imagine that a friend—call her Sarah—phones you seeking advice. Years ago, she was named trustee in another friend's will. When asking Sarah's permission to designate her, her friend explained that she didn't have candidates other than friends. She had no children of her own and was alienated from her nieces and nephews. Sarah wanted to accommodate her friend, so she gave it little thought before agreeing to be named in her friend's trust document.

Sarah's friend died last week at the age of 79. The estate in question is a mix of assets and moderately disorganized records, with nieces and nephews already making demands.

Let's consider things from Sarah's vantage point. For the first time, she's confronted with the complexities and time commitment faced by being a trustee. She's experiencing emotional turmoil, weighing loyalty to her friend's wishes against the demands of her life today.

Sarah has a full-time career and her own family to tend to. She's already very busy as it is. What seemed a minor decision years ago is today anything but humdrum. In fact, she's wondering whether to decline appointment.

Sarah says that had she known then what she knows now about the reality of being a trustee, she would have weighed her decision more thoughtfully.

She especially wishes that her friend's attorney had taken the time to speak with her in some detail at the time the will was drafted.

Estate plans routinely designate trustees, and the designation can be made many years before the named individual is asked to step into the role, in other words, at a time when there is no emotional "heat" to deal with. And, most often, the attorney drafting the estate plan gives little explanation of the day-to-day realities of being a trustee to those individuals who've agreed to be named.

So—You've Been Asked to Serve as Trustee

If you are in Sarah's position, or may be at some point in the future, how do you even begin to think about this request and whether to say yes?

Your initial response should likely be some version of, "Thank you for asking. I take your request seriously, so please give me a little time to think about it." Also ask for a copy of the trust document and answers to these questions:

- Who is the creator of the trust?
- Who are the beneficiaries?
- When would I begin to serve as trustee? Right away? When someone dies? Some other time?
- What led you to ask me?

Find a quiet place, take a few deep breaths, and tune in to your intuition. Don't overthink it as you consider:

- What does my gut tell me? Am I feeling anxiety? Excitement? Fear? Joy?
- Why am I inclined to say "no"?
- Why am I inclined to say "yes"?

We'll come back to these questions again.

Now for Some Homework

Read the trust document with purpose and curiosity. Mark it up with comments and questions. It's surprising how many people fail to do this.

A word of caution. Much of the trust document will be boilerplate (standard language to save taxes, administer the trust, and so on). Boilerplate tends to be legalese and boring. Don't skip over it. As we saw in Chapter 5's "treasure hunt," you never know what might be hidden there.

Here are some questions for you to keep in mind as you read:

- Are you able to discern the purpose of the trust?
- When would your role as trustee become active?
- Is there more than one trustee?
- What property is governed by the trust?
- Who is entitled to receive distributions from the trust? Under what circumstances are distributions to be made?
- When does the trust come to an end? Then what happens to the trust assets?

This is also the point to ask yourself some important questions. We talked in Chapter 4 about narratives. What narrative do you bring to the potential role of trustee? Are you yourself a beneficiary or a recipient of wealth? What narrative do you hold about family wealth? Do you see it as something positive or as a source of dysfunction? How do you feel about your management of your own affairs? Do you enjoy keeping track of your own assets, liabilities, income, and expenses? Or do you find such financial administration and management a real chore? Have you set up trusts for or made significant gifts to your own children or other relatives? If so, did that go well or not so well? Giving yourself honest answers to these questions is a key part of approaching potential trusteeship with open eyes.

If You Are New to the Trustscape

Once you've looked into or reflected on the questions above, if you still want to move ahead, make a list of people you know who are (or have been) trustees and/or beneficiaries. If none come to mind, ask your friends for names. Schedule times to speak with at least a few of those on your list. Listen carefully and take notes during your interviews.

Questions to ask trustees might include:

- How did you make your decision to accept appointment?
- What has your experience been serving as a trustee? What's challenged you the most? What's surprised you the most? What's given you the most satisfaction?
- What advice do you have for me?

Questions for beneficiaries include:

- How would you describe a great trustee?
- What works really well between you and your trustee? What could stand some improvement?
- What advice do you have for me?

When your interviews are complete, ask yourself these questions once again:

- What does my gut tell me?
- Why am I inclined to say "no"?
- Why am I inclined to say "yes"?

Understanding the Technical Side

Assuming that you are still on board, the next step is to ask the trust creator to schedule a time for the two of you to speak with the attorney who drafted the trust document. An hour should be enough. Your goal is to understand, at a high level, the trust document, the trustee's legal duties, possible liabilities, the advisory team, and the magnitude and complexity of assets. Don't forget to bring the copy of the trust document that you marked up.

A word about liability: in discussions of trusteeship, liability often becomes the central topic, if not the only topic, of consideration. This is unfortunate, since the point of trusteeship is to serve well, not to protect yourself. That is why we have focused our attention on the larger, human questions of trusteeship rather than the technical matter of liability.

That said, liability is an important concern, and it would be rash to enter into trusteeship without giving it thoughtful consideration. Generally, when a trust benefits private individuals alone (and not charitable entities), the main source of liability arises from claims that those individuals, the beneficiaries, may have that the trustee has harmed their interest by inadequate administration, poor investment oversight, or unfair distributions. It is impossible to predict all specific *occasions* for such claims. But if you are considering accepting appointment as a trustee, here are some questions that may highlight *conditions* in which claims against you might arise:

- Do you know the beneficiaries or are they strangers to you?
- Did the trust creator have a close or a strained relationship with the beneficiaries?
- Does the family have a history of conflictual relationships with each other? Is there a history of "cutting off" family members when conflict has arisen?
- Does the family have a history of litigation? In particular, are there any instances of past trustees being sued?
- Will you be dealing with beneficiaries who are children from multiple marriages? If so, have there been amicable or conflictual relations among the various spouses and ex-spouses?
- Will you be dealing with beneficiaries from multiple branches of the family?
- Will you be dealing with beneficiaries from multiple generations?
- Do you know if any of the present or future beneficiaries have or have had significant addictions or other behavioral issues?
- Does the trust include assets that require special expertise to manage?

- Does the trust direct the trustee to take any unusual steps with regarding to managing certain assets (e.g., holding a particular stock despite adverse market conditions)?
- Does the trust hold some or all of the ownership in a family business?

None of these conditions (except perhaps a history of litigation) is a proverbial "red flag." But they are all potential "yellow flags," which would counsel you to go slowly and ask more questions before accepting appointment.

Following the meeting with the attorney and your reflection on these matters of liability, once again ask yourself:

- What does my gut tell me?
- Why am I inclined to say "no"?
- Why am I inclined to say "yes"?

Almost There

This set of questions for yourself takes it deeper:

1. Do I understand why the trust creator selected me to be trustee? More importantly, do I believe the trust creator's reasoning in choosing me to be a trustee was valid?
2. Am I sufficiently humble about areas where I'm inexperienced, and ready to take initiative to inform myself through reading and consulting with others or expanding my experience at my own initiative?
3. Am I comfortable overseeing the spending choices of the beneficiaries? Do I think that monitoring a family member's money could change my relationship with them?
4. Do I know what to do if there is a difference of opinion between me and the beneficiary? With whom would I consult? Have I identified friends/colleagues who could

advise me informally who are otherwise independent of the
trust and its beneficiaries?

5. Have I talked with the beneficiary about the implications of
   this new arrangement, goals, and expectations?
6. Am I looking forward to the opportunity to be trustee for
   this family member? If so, why? How will they benefit?
7. Will I be paid for this work? If so, how do I feel about that?
   And how will my compensation be determined? If not, how
   else might this effort benefit me?
8. How significant do I think the liability risk is? Am I comfortable with the liability associated with becoming a trustee?
9. Am I prepared to take on the long-term commitment of
   being a trustee? If I ever believe it is right or necessary to step
   down, what is the process for resigning?

A Final Step

At this point, you may be asking yourself: "Why would anyone
ever agree to serve as a trustee?" After all, don't the time
commitment, administrative responsibilities, and potential liability add up to a terrible burden? If that's all there is to being a
trustee, we'd tend to agree—and advise you to leave it solely to
the professionals.

So, before you make your decision, we suggest a final step.
Now's the time to rise above administrative responsibilities and
use your imagination. Read a handful of the inspiring stories in
TrustWorthy.[1] See if you can imagine yourself stepping into the
life-changing roles played by the trustees. Does that impact your
"narrative" about serving as trustee?

Now You're Ready to Decide

Some people accept appointment as trustee because they view
trusteeship as a meaningful way to serve their family or a friend.

There are those who accept because they don't want to let family or friends down. Others have declined because of the emotional or time commitment, or the potential liability, or the fear that serving in that role will change their relationships in possibly negative ways. There is no right or wrong answer. Do your research, and then follow your heart.

One more point: in Chapters 7 and 8 we discussed the choices that you may have with regard to *selecting* trustees or trust protectors. This chapter has focused on considerations before *accepting* appointment as trustee. If your focus is selection rather than acceptance you can also use many of these same questions for evaluating possible candidates for these roles. And if a trustee candidate comes to you with these questions in hand, that's a good sign that he or she is evaluating the possibility of serving with great seriousness.

Note

1. Goldstone and Wiseman, *TrustWorthy—New Angles on Trusts from Beneficiaries and Trustees*. Trustscape LLC (2012).

Chapter 10

Creating Preambles

Many of us beyond a certain age, if asked to define "preamble," will harken back to sixth-grade civics, and start with an example—and three powerful words: "We the People . . ."

The Preamble to the United States Constitution conveys the fundamental purpose of what's to follow. In general terms, it states what the founding fathers hope the Constitution will achieve:

> We the People of the United States,
> in Order to form a more perfect Union,
> establish Justice,
> insure domestic Tranquility,
> provide for the common defense,
> promote the general Welfare,

and secure the Blessings of Liberty to ourselves and our
Posterity,
do ordain and establish this Constitution for the United
States of America.

It would've been odd had the drafters begun the Constitu-
tion with Article I, talking about the Senate and House of
Representatives. Readers would wonder, "What's the point?
Where are you taking us, and why?"

Yet attorneys who draft trust agreements do this all the time.
Trusts lead off with the name of the trust, its date, its term, or
some other bit of information. Interesting to know, but the
reader is left wondering about the purpose of it all.

Naturally, a trust agreement isn't the U.S. Constitution, but
the same principle applies when it comes to a family's principles
and purposes.

Preambles and Purpose

A family may be engaged in estate planning from scratch. Or they
may be living under the "governance" of older trusts. In either
case, sharing some clarity about the purposes of a trust will have a
long-term positive impact on the people affected by it.

While trustees are, of course, bound by the language of the
trust agreement, in practice they recognize that "knowing what
the trust creator would have wanted" provides valuable guidance
in making decisions. And you shouldn't have to infer or deduce
the intent by splitting hairs about the content.

Trustees and beneficiaries alike tell us that knowing that
intent is crucial. Said one beneficiary: "It was what I needed
personally to hear so that I could make sense of how and why this
was happening to me!"

The language of a trust embodies the thoughts and feelings of
the trust creator at a distinct moment in his or her life and in the

family's evolution. If the document reflects the trust creator's fears and anxieties, these disturbing dynamics are likely to impact the family for generations to come. We may hear adult beneficiaries complain that there is too much "control from the grave," or that the trustee is acting *in loco parentis* long after the beneficiary has left childhood.

In contrast, if a preamble is carefully crafted, the impact on future generations has a greater probability of being aligned with most every parent and grandparent's fondest wish—that their heirs be given the opportunity to pursue meaningful, healthy lives.

There is another significant benefit of trust creators' writing a preamble (or expressing purpose in some other way): it may prompt future trustees always to keep in mind the question that is fundamental to discretionary trust distributions: "Is this distribution enhancing the life of the beneficiary?" If that question is not part of the formal, legal language of the trust (and it probably will not be), some trustees may say, "Well, my hands are tied: I just can't consider it." However, if the trust creator includes a preamble that speaks about his or her view of what life enhancement looks like, or at the very least asks the trustee to consider this question, then while future trustees will not be *required* to do so they will be much more likely to feel *empowered* or even *encouraged* to ask that question and take it seriously.

This suggestion that you create a preamble for your trust or trusts is part of a larger movement to infuse trusts and estate planning more generally with a greater sense of purpose. Some of the other ways that trust creators are expressing purpose in or around their documents include:

- Drafting a "trust summary" to accompany each trust, summarizing the major terms of the trust and including a paragraph expressing the trust creator's intent.
- Including "text boxes" within trust documents summarizing each section and explaining why the trust includes those terms

- Writing an "ethical will" that expresses the trust creator values, life lessons learned, or perhaps the history of the wealth creation, along with the giver's hopes for what the gift accomplishes.
- Writing a short "letter" to one's descendants, describing oneself at one's best and thereby capturing the true legacy to be handed down.
- Shooting a video of the trust creator in which the giver talks about his or her life, values, and wishes.

None of these expressions of purpose is meant to take the place of the legal language of the trust; all of them are, in lawyer-speak, "precatory." They are wishes rather than commands. The preamble is just one of these forms of expression. We encourage you to think about which form or forms of expression would fit your family and your documents.

"But My Trust Was Drafted 20 Years Ago!"

Ideally, every trust would begin with a short paragraph to clarify the trust creator's intentions and set the tone. Several attorneys we know (including one of the co-authors) have for years begun each trust with a two-sentence preamble: "This trust is a gift of love. It exists to enhance the lives of its beneficiaries."

How's *that* for setting the tone? Can there be any doubt of the trust creator's intent?

Many readers of this guide have trusts. Some were probably drafted years ago, and hardly any likely begin with a preamble. That comes as no surprise. Attorneys who cross paths with the concept often are dubious. Many tell clients some version of: "I've been drafting trusts for 30 years. My trusts are bulletproof. I know how the courts will construe every word. Why should I change?"

That view shouldn't deter you. There are ways to be prudent without forsaking communication. The task is not just to understand what goes on within a trust agreement's four corners. What really matters is how those who are affected interpret a trust. How are they going to avoid misunderstanding and conflict? How are they going to promote well-being?

As we're about to see in a moment, anyone entering a trustscape, at whatever point in time, has the opportunity to create a preamble. That includes trust creators—even long after they have signed their trusts—as well as trustees and beneficiaries. It is an opportunity not to be missed.

Themes and Schemes

No matter its format, a preamble will answer three questions:

1. Who is speaking?
2. Who is being spoken to?
3. What does the speaker want to be known about the trust or the trust relationship?

If the preamble is within the trust document, it will probably be the voice of the trust creator speaking to the beneficiaries. For example:

> I've created this Trust to give you, my family, what I hope will be the best opportunity to thrive after me. I do not wish for the money I leave behind to harm your pursuit of meaningful lives; rather, I would like it and our other assets to be helpful.

As mentioned, trust creators sometimes express their intent outside of the trust document itself. For example, an ethical will or side letter offers an opportunity for the speaker to communicate his or her legacy to readers (or listeners or viewers). The writer of an ethical will often expresses some combination of family history, personal history, core cultural and spiritual values, blessings, expressions of love, wisdom learned from life's lessons, hopes and dreams for children and grandchildren, and other matters of importance.

Sometimes an ethical will takes a "formal" tone. More often, the message is conveyed in a personal style.

Letters of wishes provide the trust creator's nonbinding guidance to trustees, beneficiaries, and advisers. We've seen a variety of types:

- A letter from the trust creator to a beneficiary explaining the creator's intent in creating the trust. This may be split into multiple letters addressed to each beneficiary who is personally known to the trust creator, and another letter to generations of beneficiaries yet to be born.
- A letter of guidance to trustees. Again, knowing how the trust creator would like the trustee to approach his task is not binding, but helpful nevertheless.
- A letter from the current trustee to future trustees and beneficiaries designed to document and regenerate the spirit of the trust.

We've included a sample letter of wishes in Appendix 1 for you to see to see how others have expressed their aspirations.

Preambles Created by Trustees and Beneficiaries

Trustees and beneficiaries often enter the trustscape years after a trust has been created. The trust creator may no longer be alive. There may or may not be a record of the trust creator's intent.

Fundamentally, it need not matter. Trustees and beneficiaries are well advised to create their own preamble for how they will work together and understand the purposes of the trust. What makes their preamble special is that it is not a preamble only to the trust but also to their *relationship*. Even if the grantor's intent is clear, step back and take a fresh look. The overriding question is, "What does the trust mean for us?"

Another way that a preamble written by trustees and beneficiaries can help is when those beneficiaries are themselves the parents of young beneficiaries. Such parents are sometimes referred to as "interim" beneficiaries. The challenge of being an interim beneficiary is that you may not want the trust to play the same role in your children's lives that it does in yours. But your trustees (or co-trustees) may tell you that, as part of their duty of impartiality, they have to treat your children just the same. Working together to create a preamble that explains how you are going to resolve such conflicts is a great way for interim beneficiaries and trustees to think through a sound and fair approach, one that addresses the trustees' concern about impartiality and the parents' concerns about what is best for their children. Of course, the ideal situation is when the trust creator, perhaps in his or her own preamble, asks future trustees and beneficiaries to take exactly this step: to work together to create their own future preamble describing how they will work together around distributions to the third generation and beyond.

We've intentionally kept this subsection brief. The process of trustee and beneficiary "getting on the same page" deserves a chapter unto itself. See Chapter 12, in which a process is described for trustees and beneficiaries to align their perceptions of the trust and their expectations for working together. This process can then result in a preamble that expresses the views of the trustees and beneficiaries at this point in time. The main point here is that trust creators are not the only people who can create a preamble. Trustees and beneficiaries are well advised to set their hand to it too.

Revisit the Preamble

Preambles do not have to be a one-time deal. People change and circumstances change. What's useful today may be less so tomorrow. We suggest that trustees and beneficiaries periodically take a look at their preamble to see what remains relevant and what may have grown stale.

Even though Thomas Jefferson famously suggested that the people should come up with a new constitution every 19 years,[1] we don't suggest ripping up your trust agreement each time the new generation comes of age, even if you could. But we do suggest that you revisit the preamble at least once a decade, as well as every time there's a significant change from the status quo. Examples of that kind of change include:

- A new trustee or beneficiary comes aboard.
- A trustee or beneficiary leaves.
- A key asset such as an operating business is sold.
- A beneficiary moves into a new stage of life.
- A significant change occurs in the health of a trustee or beneficiary.

As You Begin to Create Your Preamble

Here are some words that may spark an idea or two (add to the list as you go):

Ambition
Beauty
Challenge
Community
Compassion
Courage
Curiosity
Dreams
Education
Faith
Family

Freedom
Gratitude
Honesty
Hope
Humility
Humor
Innovation
Joy
Integrity
Legacy
Love
Opportunity
Patience
Personal growth
Perseverance
Philanthropy
Pride
Risk
Security
Service
Social responsibility
Spirituality
Tolerance
Work ethic

Note

1. See Letter to James Madison, September 6, 1789: Jefferson's principle is that "the earth belongs always to the living generation."

Chapter 11

Action Steps Prior to the First Trustee-Beneficiary Meeting

T he relationship between a trustee and beneficiary begins before their first face-to-face meeting. Most often, it's up to the trustee to set the tone, especially if the beneficiary is having a trustee-beneficiary meeting for the first time.

The initial communication between a trustee and a beneficiary—whether by phone, written communication, or at the family dinner table—is an opportunity to begin. Quite often, the conversation is brief. Introductions are made and a meeting is scheduled.

If You Are a Trustee

Follow up your initial conversation with a email to the beneficiary. In this introductory note, you may want to:

1. Briefly reintroduce yourself.
2. Confirm the time and location of the first meeting.
3. Briefly describe your hopes for the relationship.
4. Explain what you plan to cover at the first meeting.
5. Invite the beneficiary to add to the agenda.
6. Invite the beneficiary to bring a list of questions for the trustee.

Here's an example of what this email could look like:

Dear _____,

I look forward to our meeting on Thursday, May 14 at 10:00 A.M. Please plan on two hours. I'd be delighted to have lunch together following our meeting if you are available.

As a reminder, we are located at 500 Main Street, Suite 1500. The entryway to our underground parking garage is at the back of our building. Please park in one of the spaces designated for our clients. Elevator "B" will take you directly to the 15th floor.

When you arrive, my assistant, John Smith, will greet you. We'll have the usual coffee, tea, and water available, along with a light midmorning snack. Do you have any preferences? How about dietary restrictions?

Your late grandfather made it clear to me that your trust is meant to help you move ahead in life. My hope is that we develop the kind of relationship that will make that possible.

Here's how I anticipate that our meeting will unfold—and please feel free to add to this agenda. Toward that end, please give some thought to what must happen during our meeting for you to leave thinking to yourself, "This was a very good meeting. We accomplished everything that I had hoped for and more."

At the outset, we'll spend time getting to know each other. I'd like to begin to learn what's important to you. I'd also like to answer questions you have about me.

Next, we'll turn our attention to your questions and concerns about trusts generally, and about your trust in particular. Sometime before our meeting, please read your trust agreement. That will make it easier for me to offer a brief overview of the document.

Then we'll spend as much time as we need to answer your questions. I'm especially interested in understanding your goals, hopes, and any concerns you have.

I'll explain the roles and responsibilities that I have as trustee. Likewise, we'll discuss your role and responsibilities as beneficiary. Then, although they won't be at this first meeting, we'll talk about the roles and responsibilities of the trust protector, the investment adviser, and the distribution committee.

Over the years, I've learned that beneficiaries often hesitate to ask questions. Sometimes they hold back, thinking, "I should know the answer to that." If you feel that way, I understand. At the same time, I encourage you to ask anyway. I'll try to answer what I can and to help get answers when I can't.

No doubt you're wondering about receiving funds from the trust. We'll spend as much time as you need discussing how you would go about making requests and how I will analyze your requests. I'll make the process transparent to you.

We'll talk about your trust's investments in whatever detail suits you. I'll show you what our quarterly statement looks like and walk you through a sample.

Our conversation will conclude by turning our attention to any remaining questions.

I've found that it's good practice to schedule a follow-up telephone call one week following our first meeting. That way, we can discuss any questions that may occur to you after you've had a chance to reflect.

Please let me know how this meeting agenda sounds to you, and what else, if anything, you would like us to cover during our meeting.

I look forward to beginning our new relationship. See you in a few weeks.

Best regards,

If You Are a Beneficiary

The trustee may be someone that you are meeting for the first time or someone that you already know—maybe even someone whom you've known all your life. Either way, it's good practice to introduce (or reintroduce) yourself in your role as beneficiary.

A well-drafted letter of introduction will set you apart. Few beneficiaries take the initiative to lay a foundation for a productive partnership. But there is no reason that you can't. Being proactive will surprise your trustee and go a long way toward getting this relationship off on the right foot. A good trustee will be just as curious about you as you are about him or her.

Before composing your letter, take time to think about your goals for the upcoming meeting. What would you like to accomplish? What needs to happen during the meeting for you to feel that the meeting is a success? What questions would you like to have answered?

Spend time reviewing your trust instrument, noting questions and concerns as you go. If you haven't tried the "treasure hunt" exercise found in Chapter 5, now would be a good time to do so.

If you have warm feelings toward the person who created your trust, spend a few moments enjoying them. Think about what the gift of a trust will make possible. Perhaps try writing a "gratitude letter" to the trust creator, even if it will never be delivered. In the letter, give details about what you are thankful for and why.[1]

If you have negative feelings toward the trust creator, toward the trustee, or toward any other aspect of your trust, acknowledge them without dwelling on them. Do your best to set your negative feelings aside for a few moments.

Bring to mind an upside—something delightful or encouraging—about your trust, no matter how small that upside seems. Quite often, one positive thought will evoke others.

Now you're ready to draft a letter or email to your trustee. We suggest that you organize your letter along these lines:

1. Take a few paragraphs to introduce yourself. Give the trustee an idea of what's going on in your life and what's important to you. Describe your aspirations and, if appropriate, how you see your trust fitting in. Now would also be a good time to express gratitude for your trust, as long as the feeling is authentic.
2. Let your trustee know of items that you would like to talk about during the upcoming meeting. Think back to your goals and questions. In effect, you will be co-designing the meeting agenda.
3. Do you intend—at this opening meeting—to ask for funds from your trust? If so, take a look at Chapter 14, which explains in detail how to request distributions in a credible manner. Your trustee will appreciate knowing about your request and having the supporting documentation in hand prior to the meeting.
4. Close your letter with a request for the agenda and other information that will help you prepare for your meeting.

Following is a sample letter or email.

Dear [Trustee],

I am excited to meet with you and [Investment Adviser] to discuss the XXX Family Trusts. Since we'll have limited time together, I am writing to propose some topics for discussion now, and to invite you both to add anything else that you'd like to speak about on the 15th.

First, I'm confirming that you and I will have about an hour to speak before [Investment Adviser] joins us, at which point we'll have another hour to meet. Is that still correct?

I would like to begin our meeting by discussing the work I have done so far to further my career, as well as my philanthropy and financial education, which will help me carry on the stewardship of my family's legacy. I would also love to share my short-term plans to continue that work.

I will present my budget for living expenses in San Francisco this year. Then, I'd like to share my plans and goals for the coming five years and their financial implications, including tuition and living expenses during the first few years of a doctoral program in early childhood learning.

I invite you to discuss how you see the trusts participating in these short- and medium-term plans and what role I might take in the coming investment conversations.

I would also like to request two distributions. The first involves a one-time reimbursement for trust-related expenses, including attorney fees, and the financial education that I have begun. The second is a request for ongoing support for living expenses in the coming year. I have prepared written requests with supporting documentation such as receipts and my budget. Would you like the requests e-mailed to you in advance, or should I wait to provide them at the meeting?

Finally, I would enjoy discussing how the two of us can best work together going forward and, when we can meet again, either in person or over Skype.

Please let me know what additional topics you would like to discuss before [Investment Adviser] arrives.

When [Investment Adviser] joins us, I would like to begin with a few questions about the trust statements. Then review the timing and amounts of my projected financial needs, and discuss how you two might align the portfolio to address those needs.

I'd also like to discuss other topics the two of you would like to cover, and then end by discussing the best way for the three of us to work together in the future.

I also want to let you know that I may be requesting additional distributions during the next 12 months outside of my living expenses, for trust-related costs such as tax preparation, attorney consulting fees, and trust education, as well as for significant career-related expenses such as professional conferences, and travel. I am uncertain of the total costs, so I have decided to wait to request reimbursement.

Please let me know if you would like to address other topics or that I bring additional supporting materials.

I'm really looking forward to our meeting. I'd also like to thank you for taking on the challenging task of managing multiple trusts for multiple beneficiaries. I know that my grandparents would appreciate it.
   Best,

As the proverb says, "The beginning is more than half the whole." Many people assume that a trust begins with the drafting of the agreement or the trust creator's signature on the final document. In truth, a trust truly begins when the trustee and beneficiary begin their work of meeting and deciding together how to take the agreement's legalese and turn it into a positive force in the beneficiary's life. We offer the suggestions in this chapter—some reflective, some purely action-oriented—to help you both "get to the beginning."

Note

1. As we saw in Chapter 7, research shows that many (but not all) people experience a variety of lasting benefits if they take time to experience gratitude regularly. Gratitude exercises can be as simple as jotting a quick note listing "three good things" going on in your life, along with a quick description of the role of others, as well as your role, in bringing about these good things. A more elaborate exercise is writing a gratitude letter to someone to whom you are thankful, and then personally reading it to them. See Robert A. Emmons, *Gratitude Works* (San Francisco: Jossey-Bass, 2013) and Martin E. P. Seligman, *Authentic Happiness* (New York: Free Press, 2002).

Chapter 12

Positive Events, Supportive Responses

Now that we have discussed accepting the role of trustee, reviewing or even creating a preamble describing the purposes of the trust, and preparing for an initial trustee-beneficiary meeting, it may seem reasonable to jump into structuring that meeting itself. However, before taking that step, we would encourage you to think about how to bring your best thinking to bear in that meeting. That is the purpose of this chapter.

In order to prepare yourself to do so, step back for a moment from trusts and trust law and think about psychology. What comes to mind when you think about researchers looking into questions of human psychology? Chances are your answer would be some version of: They're trying to find better ways to reduce or eliminate mental illness.

In other words, psychology would seem to be aimed at raising our capacity to cope with life's stumbling blocks. And you would be half correct.

A second (and, until recently, comparatively small) group of psychologists has asked a different question. They seek to know: How can we *increase* mental *health* or, as they often call it, human *flourishing?* These psychologists are more interested in how we humans, individually and in groups, go about increasing our capacity to thrive.

Over the past two decades, this second realm of inquiry has grown into a mainstream force within the field of psychology. The body of empirical research and its practical application is collectively referred to as positive psychology.

Concepts learned from positive psychology dovetail nicely with the trustscape. In this chapter, we'll introduce you to a sampling of ideas to help you, as a trustee or a beneficiary, prepare to meet with your counterpart.

Matching Mind-set to Task

Trust officer A—you'll meet her counterpart B shortly—starts her day with a look at several reports of the previous day's goings-on in her trust accounts: cash inflows and outflows, investment activity, and the like. Her trained eye sees nothing out of order.

Then she prepares for the quarterly meeting with a beneficiary that she will be hosting later this morning. A methodical look at the file, and—good, no mistakes there either.

She contemplates the impending meeting, reminding herself that it's her responsibility to be cautious and to reinforce restraint in this relationship for the long haul. Big money can mean big problems. Her motto: "Better safe than sorry."

The meeting takes place at the trustee's office. Friendly conversation is interspersed with a review of the trust's investment performance.

When the beneficiary presents a request for a distribution from his trust, trust officer A politely replies, "No," and explains why the language of the trust leaves her no choice. When the meeting is over, A is relieved that it went the way it needed to go. A potentially troublesome set of circumstances was headed off at the start.

Across town, trust officer B's day has begun in a similar manner—checking the daily reports to assure herself that no errors were made. While preparing for her beneficiary meeting, she, too, reviews the file for accuracy.

But now their routines diverge. Trust officer B takes time to think about the beneficiary and what could make the meeting successful. She reflects on other meetings, during which she's been able to contribute to a beneficiary's growth toward maturity. If she had a motto, it would be, "Be prudent, but make something good happen!"

When the distribution request is made, trust officer B describes why she would have some difficulty approving it. She asks the beneficiary: "What do you hope to accomplish by making this request?" The answer sounds sincere, if a little halting. And then: "Why is that important to you?"

The beneficiary is surprised by these open-ended questions and even more surprised by the almost 20 minutes of thoughtful back-and-forth they lead to. They're brainstorming alternative ways of accomplishing his goal. Does he have sufficient assets outside the trust? Is there a different way to look at his goal—one that would lead to a request to which trust officer B could say "yes"?

At the end of meeting, the beneficiary leaves with a new game plan—and trust officer B feels elated.

So much for our parallel stories. Now, how might we explain the trust officers' similar behaviors when precision is called for, as distinct from their behaviors that diverge while preparing for their respective beneficiary meetings?

One answer might be found in understanding *prevention-focused* and *promotion-focused* mind-sets.[1] We're in a prevention-focused mind-set when the idea is to stop bad things from happening. When in a promotion-focused mind-set, we seek advancement, growth, and gain.

Neither mind-set is inherently better than the other. Each has its place.

In our tale, both trust officers were prevention focused when scrutinizing the reports and files with an eye toward avoiding slip-ups that could lead to loss. Trust officer A kept that focus into the meeting with the beneficiary. Trust officer B, in contrast, shifted to a promotion-focused mind-set while contemplating that day's meeting.

If you are a trustee, before reading further, give some thought to a couple of questions:

1. How would each respective mind-set help and hinder your working relationships with beneficiaries?
2. Are there some situations where each might be useful?

What's important is knowing whether we can voluntarily direct our mind-set. And if the answer is yes, how do we go about doing so?

Although each of us has a default mind-set, we can indeed take steps to shift our mind-set to match the task we are tackling. We do it all the time! Planning a birthday party calls for a different kind of attitude than does preparing a tax return.

The experience of the authors is that most trustees are comfortable with a prevention-focused mind-set. This tendency is logical, given the emphasis on avoiding mistakes. Indeed, nothing in this book should imply that trustees or others should be "soft on mistakes." Awareness at all times is the best professional standard. And, to be aware of opportunities in addition to the risks, here are some tips to shift—when circumstances warrant—to a promotion focus.

First, ask yourself, "What are the signs that this is a situation where a promotion-focused mind-set would be most appropriate?"

Then do what trust officer B did. Mull over your hopes and aspirations for the upcoming meeting. Reflect on other times when you or others contributed to someone's growth and gain. Then consider: What difference would a promotion-focused mind-set make to the success of the meeting? To the beneficiary? To you? Are there other positives?[2]

Supportive Responses to Positive Events[3]

A good way for beneficiaries and trustees to break the ice toward the beginning of a meeting is to swap stories about a positive event or two that occurred following their last meeting. The episode may be trust related, but not necessarily so.

What makes a lot of sense, if you think about it, is that the degree of our happiness in the telling of an exciting news update is affected by how the other person responds.

Let's say a beneficiary blurts out to a trustee: "Those funds that I received from my trust to study abroad—you won't believe how well it all worked out! First of all, just as I had hoped, the coursework was exactly what I was looking for and more. I have a dozen ideas for what I would like to study next. And the location? Gorgeous. We hiked in the mountains almost every weekend! I've never seen such beauty. I can't wait to show you my photographs. And—can you believe it—I now have a whole new group of friends from all over the world to stay in touch with. We're already planning a reunion. . . ."

Okay, trustees, here's a pop quiz. Which of the following responses will lead to deeper connection with the beneficiary?

(a) Wow! That sounds incredible. Your hard work to get accepted into the semester abroad program really paid off. And, boy, did you take full advantage it! Tell me more. . . .

(b) That's nice.

(c) Okay, but I'm wondering if the trust's money was well spent.

(d) Let's take a look at the trust statements from last quarter.

Can we agree that the first response is best? It seems so obvious. Yet it's surprising how often trustees go into autopilot and their responses sound more like one of the three others.

Here's how researchers label each type of response given by the trustee:

(a) *Active-constructive* response. Expressing enthusiastic support. Encouraging the teller to elaborate—open-ended questions work well here. The kind of response we'd like to get back when we're the bearer of exciting news.

(b) *Passive-constructive* response. Here, the trustee gave quiet, understated support.

(c) *Active-destructive* response. The response to the beneficiary was demeaning. Can you imagine someone saying that to you?

(d) *Passive-destructive* response. The trustee ignored what the beneficiary had to say.

As you might imagine, only active-constructive responses build friendliness, trust, and openness. But that's only if your response is genuine. Don't say it unless you mean it.

So as you prepare for a meeting, does it make sense to remind yourself to pay attention to how you'll respond to good news?

Play to Your Strengths

Research has shown that playing to our strengths, as opposed to shoring up our weaknesses, will lead to greater success and life satisfaction.[4] Identifying our strengths can be challenging as, in general, many people lack a vocabulary of strengths. So we look for clues. Strengths are often at play while we are doing things that we are good at and are simultaneously experiencing an elevated energy level. Another clue is to notice when we are in a state of flow, that is, so absorbed in what we are doing that time seems to stand still; in such moments, one or more of our highest strengths are frequently engaged. Another way to spot strengths is to think about things we loved to do as a child or to ask yourself, "When do I feel most alive?" Finally, you may decide to use an empirically validated assessment to help identify your strengths.[5]

The authors suggest that a trustee pay attention to how she might employ her own strengths and draw out those of the beneficiary. Here's a several-pronged practice.

Put together a list of your strengths. Then ask:

1. How have my strengths come into play/not come into play in past meetings with beneficiaries?
2. How would they come into play if things were to go well in the upcoming meeting?
3. Do I ever fall into the trap of equating a beneficiary with his or her "problems"? Do I label that person forever as a "problem" beneficiary?
4. As I think of someone who is a "problem" beneficiary, can I list some of this person's strengths and virtues?
5. Am I surprised to discover how many strengths and virtues this person has once I begin to pay attention?
6. Suppose the beneficiary won't change in the way I wish for. What can I do to improve the situation regardless? How can I bring my strengths and virtues into play? How can I engage

the beneficiary's strengths? What difference will that make to me? To the beneficiary?

These are three examples of what we call "positive" approaches. In the real world, of course, you, the reader, are invited to make use of—amend and refine—these ideas to make the most of your own trustee-beneficiary situations.

Notes

1. Prevention-focused and promotion-focused mind-sets are the subject of research of Drs. Heidi Grant Halvorson and E. Tory Higgins, directors of the Motivation Science Center at Columbia University. See their book *Focus* (New York: Hudson Street Press, 2013).

2. Adapted with permission from Hartley Goldstone, *A Tale of Two Trustees*, which first appeared at http://wealthmanagement.com/estate-planning/tale-two-trustees. © Trustscape LLC.

3. See Shelly L. Gable et al., "Will You Be There for Me When Things Go Right? Supportive Responses to Positive Event Disclosures." Journal of Personality and Social Psychology Vol. 91, No. 5 (2006): 904–917. While the studies involve interactions between people in close relationships (romantic partners, parents, best friends), we believe there may be applicability to interactions between trustees and beneficiaries.

4. To see what a broad spectrum of research says, go to www.viacharacter.org/www/Research/Research-Findings#nav

5. A strengths assessment that the authors like is the VIA Survey, found at (www.viacharacter.org/www/The-Survey#nav)

Chapter 13

Trustee-Beneficiary Meetings

Meetings between a trustee and a beneficiary are business meetings. Treat them as such. Prepare an agenda that is agreed upon ahead of time. Plan sufficient time to move through the agenda comfortably. Hold the meeting in a setting that allows for privacy—which means somewhere other than a restaurant. Schedule social time to follow the completion of business.

Does the prior paragraph sound surprising? It probably should. Much of it is contrary to the typical practice of beneficiary and trustee meetings. The beneficiary may show up with a question or two. But apart from that, the session will likely be little more than a review of the trust's investment performance over lunch, an ample dose of polite small talk, a firm handshake, and then it's farewell until next quarter or even next year.

Premeeting Checklists

Because trustee-beneficiary meetings are serious business, they require prework. Whether you are a trustee or a beneficiary, you have some preparation to do.

For trustees, the premeeting checklist may include:

1. Review the trust instrument, correspondence, trust statement, and other notes.
2. Review the meeting agenda. What are the highest purposes of the upcoming meeting? What would great outcomes look and sound like?
3. Review your internal narratives about the beneficiary, the trust creator, and the upcoming meeting. (For a refresher on narratives, review Chapter 4.) Do these narratives serve both you and the beneficiary well? If not, what can you change to bring your narratives into alignment with the highest purposes of the meeting?
4. Review the beneficiary's distribution request(s), if any. At first glance, does the request appear to enhance, rather than merely subsidize, the beneficiary's life? What questions can I ask the beneficiary that may lead to a deeper conversation, if appropriate?
5. Big questions to reflect on, as appropriate, include:
   - Is the beneficiary self-aware? Does the beneficiary perceive the difference between courage and bullying? Between hubris and humility?
   - Has the beneficiary sought to know his or her calling? If yes, is he or she pursuing it? If no, why not?

- Has the beneficiary had a mentor in pursuing his or her calling, or in any other area of life? If not, does the beneficiary have the skills to find one?
- Can this person express compassion for him- or herself and for others? Express gratitude? Express joy and humor?
- Does the beneficiary take active roles in the larger society?
- Does the beneficiary have a process for evaluating possible advisers?
- Does the beneficiary feel and accept reciprocal responsibilities to the family? Does he or she work to instill financial and other knowledge in the next generation of the family?
- If the beneficiary requires growth in any of these areas, am I equipped, as trustee, to assist the beneficiary?

For the beneficiary, the premeeting checklist may include:

1. Review the trust instrument, correspondence, and other notes.
2. Add new questions to your written "master list" of questions for the trustee. Bring the list with you to the meeting.
3. Review the meeting agenda. Do you have anything to add? What would great outcomes look like? Does this agenda allow for these great outcomes?
4. Review your distribution request(s), if any. How would the request enhance your life? What difference would that make to you?
5. Review your internal narratives about the trustee, the trust creator, and the upcoming meeting. Be very curious as you examine your narratives. Where do they come from? Are they serving you?
6. Review your strengths. How might you play to your strengths to add to the success of the meeting?
7. Reflect upon some of the big questions for beneficiaries found in Chapter 7.

If This Is the First Meeting

The first 45 minutes or so will go a long way toward setting the stage for your relationship. As countless moms have told countless children over the years, you don't get a second chance to make a first impression. Ideally, the meeting has been prepared for with the back and forth of introductory letters of the sort we reviewed in Chapter 11.

After introductions, the first order of business at the meeting is for the trustee to break the ice with a very brief explanation of her role, a word or two about her experience and her approach. Explain the nature of the journey that the two of you are embarking on together. Pause for questions.

Next, ask gentle, probing questions designed to help both trustee and beneficiary surface and understand the beneficiary's (mis)perceptions, anxieties, expectations, and so on. Maybe try out some version of this speech:

> I never knew your grandfather, the trust creator. But if I had to guess, he probably would want your trust managed in a way that enhances your life, not simply subsidizes it. So I hope to get to know you well over time. But first, I'd love to know—what kinds of things are on your mind? What puzzles you about your trust? How about if you start by telling me what you think you know about trusts, generally, and about your trust in particular. That way, I can clear up any misconceptions. Then we'll build upon what you already know. . . .

Then address gaps in the beneficiary's understanding by supplying solid knowledge. Keep in mind that, although you may be well-acquainted with trusts, it may be unfamiliar territory for a newly-minted beneficiary. The beneficiary may be a competent adult who simply lacks facts.

Imagine being presented with a trust agreement that seems opaque. Add to that a barely-comprehensible process involving inherited money that appears to be "so near yet so far." Overlay all of this with emotion.

Here's what that may look like:

- A distraught widow, mere days after losing her husband, is shocked to learn that her financial resources will be held in trust as a result of her late husband's tax planning. The bank, as the trustee, is therefore an unexpected, and unwelcome, intrusion into her life.
- A forty-something beneficiary says: "I've been living on checks from trusts my whole life without questioning where they come from or when they will end. I'm now doing my own estate planning and thinking about my children. I have no idea how the trusts that were set up for me will affect them. And so it's time for me to grow up, and really understand my trusts."
- A successful professional in her thirties plans to bring her attorney to her first meeting with her trustees. Why? From her perspective, the trustees were an extension of her grandfather. She says: "My grandfather was a very controlling person. So was my father before he passed away. My trustees work for the family business. This feels like more of the same. I want my attorney there to balance the power."

The adviser to this latter beneficiary describes their first meeting:

For the better part of an hour, we talked about the language of the trust. Turns out that some of what she interpreted as being controlling was necessary to preserve the trust's integrity against potential challenges by her creditors: If she had been given too much authority, it could be pierced. As we talked about her assumptions, expectations and fears, she became somewhat less frustrated. The context was widening and becoming less dependent on personalities. As she gained understanding, her spirits began to lift. She no longer felt the need to bring her attorney to compensate for her feelings of powerlessness. With prompting, she talked about her gratitude for what the trust would make possible.

Only when the anxieties are reduced, and a vision for the relationship has begun to take shape, should you proceed to discuss nuts and bolts.

And our advice to new beneficiaries? Achieving trust literacy, like any branch of learning, is going to take effort. Not just study, but a rising level of awareness. You have more options than you now think. Put in the time to learn what they are.

A Sampling of Agenda Items

Toward the beginning of the meeting:

1. "What do we hope to accomplish today? What has to happen today for us to agree that this meeting was successful?" The answers don't have to be profound. Some meetings are anticipated to be little more than transactional. Perhaps the beneficiary has asked to drop by to check on the particulars of an upcoming income distribution. Nevertheless, it's good practice to ask if there's something more on the beneficiary's mind.
2. "Does the agenda look about right? Any additions or subtractions?"
3. Any significant changes in the beneficiary's life since the last meeting? Births, deaths, marriage or divorce, or new job. If so, what are the implications?
4. If to-dos were agreed upon at the last meeting, what's their status? Whatever the status, what can be learned?

Annual review:

1. What are the beneficiary's hopes, challenges, and opportunities for the coming year? Look at both big picture and specific items.
2. What are some hopes, challenges, and opportunities in the coming year for the trustee in her role as trustee?
3. Looking at the relationship, what's working well? What could stand some improvement?
4. What is the beneficiary's assessment of the trustee's performance of her roles and responsibilities to the trust and to the beneficiary?
5. What is the trustee's assessment of the beneficiary's performance of his roles and responsibilities?
6. Areas of dispute, if any: What are they? Can we resolve our differences today? If not, what are the next steps for us to take?

Technical matters:

1. Review of the trust statement, tax returns, and other "quantitative" items.

Discussions related to distributions (for more on distributions, see chapter 14):

1. Any new requests?
2. Any past requests that are still pending?
3. Any future request that we should be thinking about?

Closing items:

1. What else do we need to address before wrapping up?
2. Agree upon to-dos going forward.
3. Closing query: Did we accomplish what we hoped? What worked well? What did we learn that will be of use going forward?

An "Appreciative" Exercise

Sometimes your meetings with your trustee or beneficiary take on an especially deep level of engagement. This might be part of the agreed-upon agenda, or a sudden and new level of connection can happen on its own. The outcomes of this sort of meeting are almost always valuable to each of you. Take time during the next week or so to reflect upon as many—or as few—of the following questions as you like.

Perhaps you may wish to use both the questions and your answers as the starting point for a conversation at your next meeting.[1]

1. Think of a time when you participated in a great meeting with your trustee or beneficiary where you both were collaborating especially well. What was the situation? What was the driving force behind the success of this meeting? What were the conditions that promoted this? Specifically, what role did you, your counterpart, the physical environment, and/or the work of the meeting itself play? How did your role unleash your capacities? How did your role unleash your counterpart's capacities?

2. Think of your most recent meeting with your trustee or beneficiary. How would you rate the meeting, on a scale of 1 to 5, with 5 being the highest, in terms of engagement? What was going on that caused you to rate the meeting as high as you did (even if you chose a "low" number)? What must that meeting have looked like for you to increase your rating by 1? Who did what? With what effect?

3. Reflecting on these and other experiences, what are the core qualities and practices that bring out the best in your meetings with your trustee or beneficiary? What do you think you do well and should continue doing or do more of? What do you think your counterpart does well and should continue doing or do more of?

Mission accomplished. You did what you set out to do: comfortably worked through the "business" agenda—while at the same expanding your relationship as you learned from one another.

Now it's time to head out to your favorite restaurant for a well-deserved lunch.

Note

1. "These questions are adapted from a "solution-focused" of "brief" approach to therapy and coaching. See, for example, Berg and Szabo, Brief Coaching for Lasting Solutions. W.W. Norton & Company (2005)."

Chapter 14

Requests for Distribution

A s the prior chapter made clear, trustees and beneficiaries talk about many things, including administration of the trust, investments, taxes, as well as the trustee and the beneficiary's own lives and well-being. But probably the most charged topic of their mutual focus is distributions, the central function of a trust. In this chapter, we lay out some thoughts on how trustees can approach this delicate topic with true understanding, and how beneficiaries can prepare themselves to make thoughtful requests. To begin, we will start with one more story.

Your telephone rings. It's Susan—a middle-aged beneficiary that you have worked with for several years. Susan lives off the income from her trust. She's extremely stressed as she tells you:

I just received a letter from the IRS. They say that I owe them a lot of money! I guess I forgot to file my taxes. Even worse—I don't have enough money to pay what I owe. I'm out of my mind with worry and haven't slept for days. Can the trust pay the IRS?

Susan's trust pays income to her quarterly. That sum covers her living expenses with little to nothing left over. Principal may be invaded only for health-related expenses. Susan's health-related expenses have recently included routine check-ups and her psychiatrist's invoices.

Do you—as the trustee—honor Susan's request for funds to pay her tax deficiency?

The answer seems pretty cut and dried. You are permitted to invade principal for health-related expenses only. Susan's request is to clear up a tax matter. So you politely say "no" and explain why the language of her trust leaves you no choice.

Or do you?

Let's add a few more facts. Over the years, you have gotten to know Susan. You've learned that she's a recovering alcoholic who stopped drinking five years ago and regularly attends Alcoholics Anonymous meetings. This morning, she tells you that the IRS matter has tempted her to start drinking again.

Does this change your thinking?

This is a true story that we regularly make use of in a decision-making exercise that we developed for trustees. Invariably, participants decline Susan's request after hearing the first set of facts. After learning the additional facts, some aren't so sure.

Now, listen in to Susan's actual trust officer[1]:

I liked Susan very much. I thought this was a woman who had struggled all of her life and was trying very hard to pull her life together.

I thought about it. Maybe we had a way to say that her failure to pay taxes was making her ill. Maybe we could say that the payment for tax purposes was a medical expense.

"Would it be all right if I spoke to your psychiatrist?" I told her why.

"Yes, you may do that."

I called the psychiatrist, who said that the IRS threat was the only topic on Susan's mind. Susan couldn't get beyond it, and it might interfere with her ability to stay sober. It was awful.

"Would you write a letter to me confirming that Susan's tax situation is worsening her medical situation?" The psychiatrist readily agreed to do so.

On the basis of that letter and my understanding of Susan's plight, I agreed to pay her outstanding taxes. We also set up a system to reserve a certain amount of her trust income to pay future taxes so she wouldn't have this problem again.

This worked because I knew Susan and I thought, "Why did her mother limit the trust's ability to pay only for medical purposes?" I concluded that she was worried that if Susan got her hands on the money, she would drink it or waste it in some way. I don't think she wanted Susan to be sick because of her inability to pay taxes.

Giving Susan the money to pay taxes was the right decision.

"This Worked because I Knew Susan . . ."

When does the analysis of a beneficiary's request for funds begin? Most trustees would answer: "The analysis of a beneficiary's request for funds begins when the request is submitted." This posture is the norm, and it is logical. It is also reactive. It is one of the reasons that the distributive function of trusts is so often still-born: no one—the trust creator, the trustee, the trust advisers or protector—wants to think about distributions until a request lands in their inbox. And they may still not want to think about it even then.

We suggest that the analysis of a request works best if the process isn't reactive. Imagine the difference it will make to trustee and beneficiary if at the inception of their relationship, they deliberately begin to build a solid foundation for the analysis of requests. Over time, the trustee will come to know the beneficiary. Meetings, occasional phone calls, time spent grappling with issues both trust-related and otherwise will build trust. That, in turn, will help the trustee and beneficiary anticipate requests. And the trustee will understand the context and be in a better position to make a good decision when a request is made.

Because he knew Susan and had a pretty good idea what her mother would have wanted, when the trust officer heard Susan's request, he was armed with a narrative that (1) embraced the potential of the trust to be life enhancing and (2) was tempered with an equal dose of realism.

Granted, Susan's dilemma is out of the ordinary—and not everyone reading this will approve of the way the trust officer handled it. But this chapter, and much of this guide, is aimed at expanding perspectives and options.

Now let's tackle a beneficiary and trustee situation that's more run-of-the-mill—the request is for payment of living expenses for the coming year.

The trustee and beneficiary go through their annual ritual. The beneficiary presents a budget. The trustee reviews the budget with an eye toward the reasonableness of the expenses. Some minor negotiation and the budget is approved.

But what if a zig here and a zag there are slipped into the process?

What if a trustee asks a twenty-something beneficiary who is requesting coverage of living expenses: "If your trust were to pay your day-to-day bills, would you be giving up an important part of your independence?" This question could easily lead to a conversation about self-worth and dependency.

Or during a trustee's conversation about living expenses with a beneficiary who is further along in years: "What might you be giving up by having the trust support a certain lifestyle?" This could lead to a conversation about dialing back on lifestyle in order to have more funds available to support a favorite philanthropic undertaking.

Will either beneficiary's request or the ultimate outcomes be any different following these conversations? It is hard to say. But either way, a thought-activating conversation about what enhancing one's life really means is likely to take place.

The Request Process

There are two types of trust distributions. The first are mandatory distributions. As the name implies, the trustee *must* make mandatory distributions. Some common examples of mandatory distributions include the required distribution of annual net income to beneficiaries or the distribution of certain percentages of the trust principal to a beneficiary at a certain age (such as one-third at age 35, another half at age 45, and the remaining principal at age 55).

The other type of distributions are discretionary distributions. Again, as the name implies, the trustee has discretion over these distributions: the trustee *may* make them but does not have to. Sometimes the trust document will spell out certain standards to guide the trustee's discretion. The most common such standards are "health, education, maintenance, and support," which together are referred to by the acronym "HEMS," and which are known (for specific tax reasons) as "ascertainable standards." These words have specific meanings based on past cases in trust law. In some cases, such as in Susan's trust described above the standard is very narrow: *only* for the health of the beneficiary. In other cases the standard is very broad: the "well-being" or "comfort" of the beneficiary.

In the face of litigation from ex-spouses or other creditors, it has become more common in recent years for trusts to include no mandatory distributions and no standards to guide the trustees' discretion. This way, someone suing a beneficiary cannot argue to a court that the trustee *must* or *may* distribute trust funds for such and such purposes. If a trustee has such discretion, without standards to guide it, then the trustee is said to have "absolute discretion" and the trust is referred to as an "absolute-discretion" trust.

In what follows we are going to focus on discretionary distributions, since they involve judgment and choice. Every trustee who needs to consider discretionary distribution requests should have some sort of structure for a process for the beneficiary to follow in making requests. We have suggested the outline of such a process below:

1. Requests are made in writing. The written request will address
   (a) The purpose of the request.
   (b) The amount being requested.
   (c) The language within the trust instrument that would allow the trustee to approve the request.
   (d) The timing of the distribution.
   (e) If there will be additional requests related to this one, provide the amounts and timing of the additional requests.
   (f) Amounts and timing of other requests that the beneficiary anticipates during the coming year.
2. Supporting documents, as appropriate, should include
   (a) Invoices.
   (b) Receipts.
   (c) Budget (e.g., showing the major categories of expenses and the projected annual expenditures for each).

    (d) Business plan (in greater or less detail, depending on the experience of the beneficiary and the size of the request).

    (e) Balance sheet showing outside resources.

    (f) Other supporting documents requested by the trustee.

3. When appropriate: An essay addressing how approving the request will enhance the beneficiary's life.

4. Unless it's an emergency, requests are to be submitted according to a predetermined schedule (e.g., quarterly for smaller requests, annually for more significant distributions).

In "real life," a trustee may not require all this information for every request. Doing so would probably be quite an annoyance to the beneficiary! More likely, the trustee will work with the beneficiary to compile this information from their interactions (whether in person or over the phone) and from the trustee's own files. The goal here is not to send the beneficiary scurrying for data or to put hurdles in the way of distributions. Rather, it is to keep in mind the various questions that could help the beneficiary make the most thoughtful request possible.

Analysis of a Request

In the authors' experience, the best decisions are made when the trustee begins by discussing the request with the beneficiary. The conversation may occur before or after the formal written request is submitted. Again, such a conversation might supply a fair amount of the information needed in the formal request.

Here are some conversation starters:

- What motivates you to make this request? Is there a bigger purpose that lies beneath it?
- How does the request square with the trust creator's intent?
- How does it square with the language of the trust instrument?
- Are there more appropriate ways for you to achieve your goal other than by requesting funds from the trust?

- In addition to achieving your purpose with the help of funds from the trust, do you plan to have your own financial "skin in the game"?
- If your request is approved, what's the best possible outcome? What difference will the approval make in the short term? In the long term?
- If your request is denied, what difference will that denial make in the short term? In the long term? What would be the best possible outcome following the denial? What alternate paths might lead to accomplishing your goal?

Following the conversation and review of the formal written request, ask yourself: "Will making (or not making) the distribution be more likely (or less likely) to enhance the beneficiary's life?" As we mentioned in Chapter 10, in discussing preambles, this question probably will not appear in the trust document itself, and some trustees may feel awkward "intruding" it into the forefront of their decision-making process without the authorization of the document. It may seem like "rewriting" the document. However, if you have read this far, you would likely agree that, whether this question appears in the trust document or not, it is at the heart of the trustee's virtues of fidelity and discernment, virtues that underlie the activity of discretion. The goal here is not to rewrite existing trusts but to broaden our lens of evaluation to take into account the true breadth of possibilities and consequences of trust distributions.

Once you have considered the human question of life enhancement, then it is time to turn back to the document, and ask yourself: "Would approval of the beneficiary's request be a reasonable exercise of discretion according to the language of the trust?"

If the answers to these questions lean toward approval, there are several others to consider:

- How large is the amount of the request compared to the size of the trust? Will this request deplete the trust beyond what's prudent (or beyond what's permitted)?

- What has been the beneficiary's history of requests for the past few years? Would approving/denying this request be consistent with past decisions?
- Is the request a one-off or part of a larger plan? If part of a larger plan, what additional requests are anticipated? What would the collective impact of the requests be on the trust's assets?
- What other requests are anticipated from the beneficiary during the coming year? Beyond the coming year? How does this request potentially impact decisions that will have to be made in the future?
- What's the impact on other beneficiaries if this request is granted?
- Is the trustee required to consider the beneficiary's resources outside of the trust? If so what are the beneficiary's income, expenses, and assets?
- Is this a situation in which (if the trust document allows it) it may be better for the beneficiary to receive a loan from the trust rather than a distribution? For example, trustees sometimes make payments for a beneficiaries' residence as a loan, to be repaid the way a conventional mortgage would, rather than a distribution. It could also make sense to structure a disbursal as part-distribution and part-loan, so that the beneficiary has some "skin in the game."

Now the trustee is ready to make a decision. Once made, communicate what's been decided and the reasoning behind it to the beneficiary. Be transparent. Answer the beneficiary's questions. Address the beneficiary's concerns. If the request has been denied and the beneficiary is disappointed, offer to spend time brainstorming alternate ways of reaching the beneficiary's goals.

The last step is to document in writing the process and analysis that led to the decision. This will be a useful aid for analyzing future requests and an invaluable resource for future trustees, and it provides an important record should the decision be challenged, either in the "court of family opinion," or in a court of law.

About Enhancement

Many trusts are drafted when beneficiaries are young, maybe not even born yet. The nightmare to be protected against might look something like this:

A soon to be 21-year-old had been orphaned at a very young age, his parents killed in a tragic car accident. Growing up, many of his expenses are paid from a trust holding substantial life-insurance proceeds. Upon turning 21, the trust will come to an end and he will receive a considerable sum. Might this approaching event add firmness and a real sense of future to his perspective? In this case, no, for he happens to be immature, showing little inclination to plan beyond his payday. He tries to game the system by creatively plotting to secure an early distribution to keep his "friends" around. Within a year following his 21st birthday, the money is gone, and so are the friends.

Or, on the positive side:

A recent college grad asks for help drafting her first business plan. The conversation includes how the trust might support her dream and what would be required of her to receive financial backing. She does her homework and concludes that the idea is not sound. She goes back to the drawing board to start over again.

At the same time, it's not uncommon that the parents of "baby boomers" in their sixties are going strong in their eighties. So to think of newly-minted beneficiaries as strictly as children or emerging adults may be a disservice to beneficiaries who are further along in life. For example, does it make sense to bypass a spouse of thirty years in the chain of inheritance? Or to fail to include language permitting a beneficiary to seek funds to support a favorite philanthropic endeavor?

When performing the distributive function, we suggest that a trustee keep in mind that "enhance" depends on facts and circumstances, including the stage of the beneficiary's life. While this may seem obvious, a woman in her forties had this to say to one of the authors:

"My life is successful by almost any measure. I am a tenured professor at an Ivy League university. I have a wonderful husband and children. I sit on several non-profit boards and currently chair my family's foundation. The only place that I am treated like a child is when I visit my trustee. I have come to terms with this, but what concerns me is that my children will have to go through the same thing."

Think back to Susan's story that began this chapter. Was the trustee's approach more "partner" than "parental" because Susan was middle-aged rather than just starting out in life? When we use this story as the basis for an exercise with groups of trustees, the age that we assign to Susan does seem to make a difference.

TrustWorthy contains many examples of what enhancing the life of adult beneficiaries looks like. For example, in "We All Felt Like Godparents," thoughtful analysis leads to a decision to release funds for *in vitro* fertilization where trust language permits distribution for medical expenses only. In "Does Anybody Really Need a Helicopter," a request that on its face seems like a slam-dunk "no" leads to an affirmative decision for an executive whose business travels take him to remote, dangerous corners of the world. And in "For the Love of Siblings," a trustee takes the initiative to reunite aging brother and sister in an assisted living facility.

Note

1. From "Taxes Can Make You Sick," in *TrustWorthy*. © Trustscape LLC. Reprinted with permission.

Chapter 15

Working with Addictions

I n the prior chapters in this part of the guide, we have focused on building great relationships, particularly between the trustee and the beneficiary. Doing so involves some "internal work" as well as the "external" work of preparing for and holding meaningful meetings and productively discussing distributions. This work cuts across almost all trustee-beneficiary relationships and applies pretty much universally to trustscapes of all shapes and sizes.

In the next three chapters, we focus on more specific matters that arise within or affect these relationships, specifically, addiction, marriage, and transitions in the trustscape. These topics will not be the subject of each and every interaction between trustees and beneficiaries. But they will likely play a part, and a powerful part, in almost every trustscape at one time or another.

Helping a family member with an addiction is an incredibly difficult task. It is made all the more so when that individual has access to funds in a trust—funds that may be used to fuel the addiction even over loved ones' and trustees' concerns and objections.

Because of the specialized nature of addiction treatment and its intersection with trusts, we decided to structure this chapter as an interview with Bill Messinger, who has spent decades dealing with this topic, both as a member of a family with wealth and as a professional adviser to families. Besides being an attorney, Bill is a licensed alcohol and drug counselor. Bill's practice focuses on helping clients identify and implement winning strategies to combat alcohol and drug abuse in their families, family businesses, and beneficiaries. Interested readers can find much more on Bill's approach to managing addiction in the context of trusts at his site: www.billmessinger.com.

Family Trusts: "Bill, in your years of working with families and trustees, what are some of the major pitfalls you've seen them fall into when it comes to addiction management?"

Bill Messinger: "The first and biggest problem is with the treatment model most people use in dealing with addiction. They allow the alcoholic or addict to pick the treatment program and manage his or her recovery program. While the intention in doing so is kind-hearted, it is, unfortunately, often a recipe for failure and relapse. Also, when it comes to trusts, the language in trusts and other governance documents is usually ineffective in dealing with addiction, even when the trustee has broad discretionary authority. Finally, trustees and professionals advising families often lack training and understanding regarding addiction."

FT: "It sounds like a basic problem is the lack of understanding of effective treatment. So what works?"

BM: "The key is to apply leverage to encourage treatment compliance. The basis for this approach is the highly successful treatment programs for pilots and physicians. I will tell you a short story. My interest in developing and using the concept of leverage for trusts and families dealing with addiction began when I saw this headline in the Hazelden Voice in 1998: 'Airline Pilots Soar to Success in Recovery.' It turned out that 92 percent of airline pilots in the Hazelden program were 100 percent abstinent for two years. I did some digging and I found out that doctors also had very high recovery rates—almost 80 percent over five years. It turned out that addiction is the only field of medicine where physicians are treated differently than the rest of the population! Since that time, it has become clear to me that replicating the pilot-physician model for inclusion in trusts and other governance documents is by far the most effective way to combat substance use disorders."

FT: "Everyone has heard about high-profile cases of addiction in celebrities or high-profile families with wealth. Are the horror stories the norm? Can you say a bit about the context for addiction in families with wealth?"

BM: "Alcoholism, drug dependence, other addictions, and significant mental health disorders are statistically probable and will occur in affluent families at an estimated minimum rate of 20 percent—often much higher. These disorders will undermine the best family mission statements and succession plans and result in the loss of both financial wealth and family cohesion. Addicts and alcoholics are people with an illness. They need educated, active family members to help them find effective treatment and encourage them to engage in post-treatment recovery activities, just like relatives who are sick with other chronic, life-threatening diseases."

FT: "Why do you stress the concept of 'leverage'?"

BM: "Because without it usually nothing changes. When a doctor is addicted, the state medical board will use his or her license as leverage: comply with a treatment plan or you can't practice medicine! It is all well and good to discuss highly successful recovery programs, systems transformation, and clinically appropriate and respectful treatment to improve outcomes. But, first, a family must first overcome a basic problem: how do we get the addict to enter treatment and remain active in a post-treatment program? Without applying leverage, most addicts will continue to drink, use drugs, and continue other addictive behavior because their money and other resources buffer them from the consequences of their addiction. Unfortunately, I know people in these situations who stop only when they are institutionalized or dead."

FT: "Does using leverage mean cutting someone off?"

BM: "It may mean cutting them off from all funds *except* for funds to be used for treatment and support, as directed by a licensed counselor. Leverage never means cutting someone off from support or from contact. As painful as it may be, it is important for a family to remain engaged with an addict."

FT: "How would you recommend families approach the challenge of making their trusts secure in the face of addiction?"

BM: "First, I would say don't wait: it is not necessary to wait until someone is deeply addicted before taking action. In fact, it may be nearly impossible to help once an addiction has become deeply ingrained. Second, I do think it is important to include specific provisions regarding addiction in planning documents or to reform trusts in order to include such provisions. Third, families should use experts to evaluate members with a problem and make objective recommendations. Fourth, use requests for funds as an opportunity to learn about the problem, evaluate the beneficiary, and start to put in place a recommended plan. Fifth, be mindful of the court of family opinion as well as the court of law. Dealing with addiction or potential addiction is not a quick fix. It is not just a matter of hiring the right lawyer. It is a process that will eventually involve multiple family members and external experts. But if pursued as a process, it really can work."

FT: "You emphasize the role of experts. Families are often hesitant to invite in outsiders, even experts, especially around something as sensitive as addiction. What would you say to them?"

BM: "First I would remind family members that addiction is a chronic disease, not a personal failure. It requires a medical perspective to treat it effectively. Also, treating addiction is not a matter of 28 days and you're done. My experience is that it is more likely a two- to five-year process of recovery. Most lawyers, trustees, and family members do not have the time or the skills to help a family member with addiction navigate that process. It usually doesn't happen without the support of a trained, respectful professional."

FT: "What would a treatment approach based on the wise use of trusts look like?"

BM: "There are a couple of tracks to such an approach. First is the leverage track. On this track, it is important to have explicit leverage: expectations that are set out in governing documents such as trusts. That language may, for instance, require specific testing and treatment activities. [For examples of such language, see Appendix 2.] To get it into documents may require decanting or reforming those trusts. At the same time, non-explicit leverage is also important: I mean the sort of 'soft' leverage that can come from personal conversations, expressions of concern, and demands for change. The second track is recovery management. Here, the involvement of an expert case manager is crucial, to identify treatment options and set clear guideposts and expectations for the family and the member with the disease. This process requires clear communication among all the parties. It can also help to have a signed contract between the family members with the addiction and the rest of the family—just as doctors with addiction have to sign with their medical board. Such communication and clear delineation of expectations, as well as the involvement of an expert case manager, help take pressure off the trustees as well as other family members."

FT: "Is there language that you recommend families use as 'explicit leverage'? Is it enough to give trustees absolute discretion in making distributions?"

BM: "I don't think relying on absolute discretion is enough. The reality is that most trustees don't have the time or expertise to identify addiction problems in beneficiaries, so they may unwittingly go along with harmful requests. Also, just saying 'no' is really not sufficient, especially in the face of an insistent (and perhaps legally armed) beneficiary. That is why I recommend specific language to support that leverage. For example, give trustees the discretion to withhold distributions when beneficiaries exhibit addictive, compulsive, or destructive behaviors, mental health conditions, or any combination thereof. Give the trustee the power to withhold funds until the beneficiary is in treatment and to spend funds on treatment and licensed expert oversight of the process. Very importantly, the leverage language should also require the beneficiary to comply fully with treatment recommendations and to sign releases allowing the trustee to review treatment plans and speak with counseling staff. Finally, the documents should specify that the trustee (not the addict) has the power to select a reliable drug testing service and to withhold distributions if the beneficiary fails to comply with the recommended testing regimen."

FT: "Are there any examples of specific language that you've found helpful in trusts?"

BM: "Yes, for example, here's a case where the grantor wanted to give the trustee the direction to withhold distributions specifically in the case of addiction:

> Notwithstanding the foregoing, the trustee, in his/her sole discretion, shall withhold distributions of assets, income, or other withdrawals from any beneficiary who has an active drug and or alcohol dependency. Such assets, income, or withdrawals shall be retained and held by the trustee until such time as the trustee determines, in his or her sole discretion, that the beneficiary is in recovery from such drug and or alcohol dependency.

A second example description for the 'trigger' for withholding distributions is somewhat broader:

> If at any time a Beneficiary eligible to receive net income or principal distributions, in the sole judgment of the Trustees, is deemed to be incapable of properly managing his or her financial affairs, or should the Trustees become reasonably concerned regarding the moral conduct or affairs of any Beneficiary hereunder to such a degree as to be concerned for such Beneficiary's health or welfare, or should any Beneficiary be convicted of a crime, or be the subject of a criminal investigation . . .

And here is a third case, in which the grantor expresses very general wishes for the beneficiaries' well-being:

> It is my wish that my Independent Trustees consider (my child's) mental and physical condition and (my child's) best interests before making such distribution.

Readers can find much more extensive sample language for inclusion in trusts on my web site [and in Appendix 2 of this guide]. Naturally, the exact language will depend on the values of the grantor and the dynamics of the family. I would add that this language can be used not only in trusts but also in such shared entities as family limited partnerships or limited liability companies."

FT: "What about once a family member has entered treatment or has graduated from a program? Are there specific provisions that are helpful to have in place then?"

BM: "Absolutely. Again, treatment and recovery are not a matter of a few weeks or even months. Generally, it takes a minimum of two years for the brain to stabilize and for a person with an addiction to learn new habits. The trustee should have the power to require testing during this period and to withhold funds—except for treatment—if the beneficiary does not comply. Also, the trustee should be careful to identify the start of 'recovery' as when the beneficiary truly returns to a normal living arrangement, not when he or she is in the protective environment of a halfway house or inpatient facility. Sometimes addicted beneficiaries will threaten their spouses with loss of funds if they report their addiction, so the trustee should have the power to get funds to an addicted beneficiary's spouse or children despite the addicted beneficiary's objections. Naturally, during the period that the trustee has suspended distributions, the beneficiary should lose any power to remove or replace the trustee or act as a trustee. Finally, the trustee and the experts the trustee hires should have no liability for the actions or welfare of the beneficiary; this provision should protect the trustee and others involved from any threats by the beneficiary."

FT: "Bill, your perspective is so helpful. Do you have any final thought to share with our readers?"

BM: "Most simply, be persistent and proactive. I hope that I've encouraged trustees, family members, and their advisers to take a proactive approach in addressing substance use. Success is possible. In cases where addiction is not currently present in families my additional hope is that these thoughts will provide an impetus for families to adopt measures to effectively address dysfunctions in future generations. For far too long, beneficiaries have been suffering unnecessarily, some dying preventable deaths, to our sorrow."

Again, for sample language that Bill suggests using in trusts and similar instruments, please see Appendix 2.

Addiction may seem to be a specialized topic but this entire book is about using trusts to enhance the lives of beneficiaries, and the great danger that trusts pose is the danger of "distribution addiction," that is, addiction to monthly or quarterly support payments that sap the beneficiary's sense of purpose and striving. Seen in this light, the work of every trust creator, trustee, and beneficiary should be the avoidance of addiction. The key to doing so is to breathe life into these relationships—to give all parties a voice and a sense of dignity—so that addiction to financial distributions never usurps the beneficiary's own sense of purpose.

Chapter 16

Trusts and Marriage

s Freud observed long ago (and many songwriters remind us to this day), some of the greatest challenges people face involve love and money. When trusts intersect with plans for marriage (or remarriage), these challenges come together into one. It is no surprise that the intersection of trusts and marriage is one of the trickiest points to navigate in the trustscape.

Marriage is something that changes and evolves throughout an individual's and a family's life. So we will take up this topic from several different angles. (And by "marriage" here we mean to include any committed, long-term relationship.) First, we will consider how to manage the place of trusts as you enter into marriage. Then, we will turn to how couples can discuss trusts in their marriage, and more specifically to the question of when and how to tell beneficiaries about the existence of a trust. Finally, we will look at the thorny topic of trusts in a second marriage or beyond. Throughout, we will also be cognizant of the part that fiscal inequality between partners—especially when the woman has more wealth than the man—plays in managing the place of trusts in a relationship.

Prenuptials

Prenups are typically objects of dread to all involved. They evoke images of overly protective parents, infantilized children, gold-digging fiancés, a black mark on a new relationship, mistrust where there should be love, and suspicion where there should be hope—in short, a whole panoply of fears.

It does not have to be so. As we describe more fully in *The Cycle of the Gift*, thought and care can turn the prenup process from a nightmare into a ritual of welcome, part of the creation of the new couple and the new family. We will summarize the ways to do so below. But, first, it is crucial to recognize that trusts can play a large part in making that process positive, rather than adding to its negativity.

The reason is that if the trusts are structured correctly, the trust assets may not be part of the to-be-formed "marital estate" belonging to the new couple. In many states and countries, the trust assets would simply be "off the table" with regard to a possible divorce or dissolution, and so would not have to be the subject of negotiation in the prenup process.[1] They must be disclosed, both for the integrity of that process and, more importantly, for the education of the beneficiary and his or her potential life partner. But disclosure does not equal access, much less distribution. The trust assets are part of the landscape for the new family, but not part of the ground that belongs to them or that they might one day have to divide.

The presence of trusts prior to the prenup process can, as a result, provide the marrying couple some relief. We have heard many beneficiaries say that they felt relieved that their parents had put assets into trust, since it removed any decision about those assets from their—the young family members'—hands. As one fiancée said, "I didn't feel like I was telling my boyfriend that I didn't want him to have this property. I was able to say that the decision was made long before he came along." Likewise, a fiancé once told us, "I was glad to learn that her assets were in trust. That was her dad and mom's gift to her. It had nothing to do with me. She and I could then make our life together and I could make my gift to her myself." It also helps to frame the use of trusts in terms of the family's values and history rather than as part of a plan to protect against this or that spouse. For example, some families have explained, "This is simply what our family does: it's not about you." Or similarly, "Our family wealth (or business) is a family asset that affects many different people and is part of our legacy. That's why we put these assets into trust."

These examples also show how often trusts are part of the larger dynamic of fiscal inequality. Fiscal inequality in a marriage is a big topic, which goes beyond the scope of this chapter. It is also a topic that is becoming more and more common, as parents make lifetime gifts to their children and as women, in particular, find themselves in possession of more and more wealth. The key to managing such inequality is empathy for the other party and for oneself. Recognizing the challenge that inequality poses within a relationship, for both parties, is the start to their managing that inequality. From that empathy flows the ability to communicate and to talk about what the difference means for each of them. Such differences become much more manageable when each party is clear about his or her own feelings and has put those feelings "on the table."

As mentioned earlier, communication is also crucial for managing the prenup process as a whole, with or without the presence of trusts. Condensed to its simplest form, that communication process involves some or all of these steps:

1. As a family, getting clear which—if any—assets each child brings to the marriage (that is, which assets are not already disposed via trusts).
2. As parents of a marrying adult child, clarifying what your feelings are about a prenup and what motivates your feelings (this is particularly important if Dad and Mom perhaps differ with each other about the topic).
3. As parents, deciding whether you are willing to leave the decision about a prenup in the hands of your child.
4. As a fiancé or fiancée, clarifying what your feelings are about a prenup and what motivates those feelings.
5. Between parents and child, communicating your feelings clearly with the goal of understanding and empathizing with each other.
6. Between fiancé and fiancée, communicating your feelings clearly with the goal of understanding and empathizing with each other.
7. Based on these steps in communication, deciding on how the prenup process can best support the formation of the new marriage.

As with any process of communication, some people are more adept at it than others. In particular, it may be challenging for marriage & family lawyers who look at the prenup process through an adversarial lens to help family members use the prenup process in a positive way. In such situations we have seen families make good use of "translators": people with expertise in trusts and family dynamics who have been able to help the family clarify their positive intent and then "translate" that intent to both sets of marriage & family lawyers. This "translation" can save a great deal in hurt feelings, anxiety, and legal fees.

The prenup process is never easy, but if pursued with goodwill, it can produce much better results than bottling up the anxiety and then posing the demand for a prenup shortly before the nuptials. Indeed, when motivated by positive purpose (rather than as an expression of fear), the prenup process can serve as part of "onboarding" of the new spouse into the family rather than seem to be a locked door or sign of suspicion at the beginning of the marriage. Again, our main point here is that the presence of trusts—far from making the matter more difficult— can actually ease the process and help put the focus less on property and more on the happy couple and their new marriage.

Within Marriage

There are many ways that trusts can impact an established marriage. For example, couples, one or both of whom are beneficiaries of family trusts, may revisit the question of how much or how little to integrate those trusts into their marriage. This work amounts to revisiting and perhaps renegotiating the prenup process in the context of an established marriage. Also, couples who are setting up their own family trusts need to decide how much of their property to put in trust, for whom, and under what terms of distribution. Even more basically, they need to decide how to decide these matters: will both of them have an equal say, or will the spouse who has created the wealth take the lead? In the heat of creating wealth and raising children, many couples "default" to the latter approach, leaving the wealth-creating spouse (often, but not always, the husband) to work out the "legal details" with little input from the other spouse. If that happens, they may want to revisit those details in later years, when they have more time and experience to reflect on their prior choices.

For the sake of brevity, we focus here on the challenge that married couples typically struggle with most when it comes to trusts that they have established during their marriage: the question of what to tell their growing children about the trusts and when to tell it.

This, too, is a topic that we take up more fully in *The Cycle of the Gift*. Here, we condense the material to its essence, while adding considerations specific to trusts as distinct from family wealth more generally.

To answer this question, we recommend that couples take the approach first recommended by our friend and colleague Charles Collier, former senior philanthropic adviser at Harvard University (and also described in Chapter 7 in the section on trust creators). Charlie called this approach the "three-step process." It has helped countless couples navigate difficult decisions; it amounts to the following:

1. First, each member of the couple should clarify what he or she wants to communicate; what are the goals, from his or her perspective, of the communication; and how he or she feels about communicating with his or her children about the trust.
2. Second, with this individual clarity in mind, the two members of the couple should share their thoughts with each other, with a goal first not of "winning over" the other but rather of listening, learning, understanding the other's point of view, and empathizing with the other partner.
3. Third, only when the couple has fully explored step 2 should they move on to deciding, as a couple, what they want to communicate to their children, when, and how.

Typically, we see couples skip steps 1 and 2 and try to move directly to step 3, especially by trying to answer the "when" and "how" questions. That is why those questions often feel so insuperable: because the members of the couple may not know their own hearts, much less what's going on in the other's heart and mind. In contrast, if a couple devotes time and energy to steps 1 and 2, step 3 moves relatively quickly and smoothly.

Of course, there are at least two sides to every communication. The parents are one side. Children are the other. And sometimes parents have good reasons for doubting their children's ability to hear, understand, and integrate, in a healthy way, information about family trusts. The concerns about trusts' demotivating children's work ethic are real.

The answer to such concerns, which are very common, is to seek to understand each child as an individual. Some children are almost naturally responsible and self-directed: they may be able to understand and integrate information about trusts in a healthy fashion even when they are in their late teens. Other children may find it difficult to integrate such information even in their late 20s or 30s. Most children are probably somewhere in between.

Parents often take one of two approaches to this situation. The first is secrecy. They withhold information about the trusts as long as possible, perhaps even long after their adult children are legally entitled to receive this information. Or parents establish their trusts in jurisdictions that do not require notifying adult beneficiaries of the trust's existence. As tempting as it is, we have rarely seen this approach work out well. It creates a large opportunity cost: the time spent keeping things secret could have been used to educate the beneficiary in the ways that we discuss elsewhere in this book. It also almost always breeds resentment. The truth will out at some point. The adult beneficiary will then tally up all the ways that knowing the truth earlier could have influenced his or her life choices. Whether or not his or her retrospective assessment is accurate, the resentment at being treated like an irresponsible child will be real and damaging.

The other customary approach is to punt the entire discussion and place it in the hands of an "expert," usually an officer of the institutional trustee (if there is one) or the professional trustee (such as an attorney). This occasion usually comes out of the blue for the beneficiary, creating anxiety, which is hardly a good foundation for learning. The discussion also tends to be technical and one-sided. Beneficiaries often leave such meetings feeling bewildered and even ashamed. The result may be that the entire subject is dropped for years or decades more. That may be the result that some parents wish for, but, again, it sets up a dynamic that usually ends in poorly educated, poorly prepared beneficiaries. As the old adage says, "Failure to prepare is preparing to fail." With this poor "preparation," it should be no surprise that so many beneficiaries do not succeed to manage their trusts well.

Instead, as we described in Chapter 7, we recommend tailoring the communication to beneficiaries based on who those beneficiaries are. Sometimes that process may involve the step of having a third party actually interview each adult beneficiary to learn what his or her level of knowledge is, how prepared each person is to learn about the trust, and what questions he or she has about the topic. Such interviews can be a great way to prepare beneficiaries to get the most out of the process as well as to prepare parents and their advisers to teach beneficiaries most effectively. These interviews can also help parents decide whether to share information with their children as a group or as individuals, with their spouses (if the children are married) or without.

Whatever the communication process ends up looking like for you—whether it is as simple as a few one-on-one conversations or as involved as the series of interviews and planning sketched out above—we return to this fundamental principle: seek to understand. If you use each interaction with your children as a chance to learn about who they are, what they know, what they would like to know, and how well they are likely to integrate that knowledge, then the "what," the "when," and the "how" of your communication will likely flow quite naturally.[2]

Second Marriages and Beyond

There is nothing as complex in family life as blended families, whether that blending comes about after the death of a prior spouse or through divorce. The presence of trusts within the family adds complexity upon this complexity. Managing the dynamics of trusts and remarriage requires great delicacy, patience, and empathy by and for all parties.

There are many permutations that this complexity can take. One, for example, is when a spouse dies after setting up a "marital trust" for his or her surviving spouse, and then that surviving spouse remarries. This situation bears some resemblance to the situation of young people marrying for the first time with family trusts in the background. It can cause some anxiety in the remarrying spouse and his or her new companion. But it can also be a source of relief: the marital trust established by the deceased spouse likely has clear terms about distribution and use of the assets. It is probably "off the table" in the new marriage. This status may help the new couple create their own economic world, with as few feelings of guilt or resentment about the deceased spouse's role in their economic life as possible.

Marital trusts also play a role in perhaps the most common and most difficult situation involving trusts and remarriage: when a person with children remarries and creates a marital trust for his or her new spouse. The situation is made all the more challenging if the new spouse is much younger than the trust creator. Sometimes that new spouse and the children from the prior marriage may even be close to the same ages.

In such cases, it is natural for the children from the first marriage to wonder about the new spouse's motives: is he or she just marrying Mom or Dad for the money? It is also natural for the children from the first marriage to worry about the consequences for themselves and their children: Will the wealth outlive the new spouse? Will there be anything left for us?

Will we have to wait all our lives? These are not particularly noble concerns, but they are common ones.

Again, these are situations of great complexity, and simple answers would not do them justice. However, in working with many families, we have observed one rule: it is generally much better to address these matters while you are alive than to leave them to be hashed out between your adult children and your second wife or husband after you are dead.

The reason is simple: while you are alive, you and your new spouse can formulate your reasons for establishing the marital trust and communicate those reasons to all interested parties. Children from a prior marriage may be pleased for you, or they may be resentful and angry. That is their choice. But at least they will be informed. They will know your thoughts and feelings. There will be no room for complaining later about what Dad or Mom "would have wanted" or "really thought."

The three-step process of communication described earlier is the same one that we recommend spouses in a second marriage use to clarify their thoughts and feelings about communicating about trusts with children from prior marriages. This process would also cover thinking about whether you want to leave assets in trust for children from your spouse's prior marriage, which sometimes happens in second marriages where there is considerable fiscal inequality between the partners. Whatever you decide in such situations, the key is that you and your spouse clarify your own individual thoughts (step 1), share those thoughts honestly with each other (step 2), and then decide what you are going to do or say (step 3).

This process is much easier said than done. It may be important, for example, to incorporate a values-clarification exercise as part of steps 1 and 2. Such an exercise would allow the two spouses to clarify what matters most to each of one of them and what values they hold in common. Recognition of their differences and their common ground would then provide a firmer basis for thinking through actions and communication.

This entire process will take time, especially if there is lingering anger and resentment within the family due to earlier conflict or divorce. The situation is particularly difficult if you fear that communicating your wishes regarding your new spouse to your adult children will cause them to "hold hostage" your relationship with your grandchildren. This is a terrible situation for a grandparent to be in. In such cases, it is all the more important to talk through the situation with your new spouse, so that you both are clear about the pros and cons of different approaches, the benefits, and the likely costs. Sometimes one must let the proverbial chips fall where they may, but only when they must. If that is the case, it is crucial that the couple be clear about that course of action and that they agree on the reasons for proceeding—or for not proceeding—with communication.

Again, love (and especially parental love) often brings us our greatest joys and greatest pains, and money can serve to intensify both. There are no easy answers for navigating the role of trusts within a marriage. However, we have found that when couples, young or old, take the time to understand themselves, each other, and their children, the steps that they take, even if sometimes painful, generally produce a more positive result.

Notes

1. The treatment of irrevocable trusts in divorce is a constantly changing field and it requires careful legal consideration. Within the United States, some states have moved to make trusts even more resistant to division as marital property, while other states have moved in the opposite directions. The case is the same on the international scene. For insight into the situation in your jurisdiction, please seek competent legal advice.

2. In addition to *Cycle of the Gift*, there are many other good discussions of best practices in communicating with children about wealth. When it comes to young children, a particularly insightful treatment is *Mommy, Are We Rich?* by Suzen Peterfriend and Barbara Hauser (Mesatop Press, 2001).

Chapter 17

Transitions

Solomon's Ring

There is a story told of King Solomon, who was known for his wisdom. Solomon wanted to test the ingenuity of his chief adviser, his grand vizier. Solomon had a birthday approaching in a few months, so he called his vizier to him and said, "This year I want you to find me an especially rare and wonderful present: something that can make a happy man sad and a sad man happy."

For weeks the vizier racked his brain as to what to give his master. But while he could find plenty of things to make a happy man sad, and even a few things that might make a sad man happy, he could find nothing to do both. At last as the big day approached, the vizier found himself wandering miserably through the Great Bazaar. His eye then fell upon an item in the corner of a merchant's humble stall. After examining it for a moment, he knew that he had found his prize.

On his birthday, assuming that the grand vizier had failed, Solomon asked him to step forward with his gift. The vizier did so and placed a simple silver ring in his master's palm. Solomon was surprised. "What is this?" he demanded.

"Master, read what it is inscribed upon it," quietly replied the vizier.

Inscribed on the outside of the ring were the words "This Too Shall Pass."

"Remember it, O Wise One," said the vizier to his master, "in your moments of happiness and in your moments of sadness." Solomon smiled and knew that his adviser was at least as wise as he.

This Too Shall Pass

It is a saying worth remembering by trustees, beneficiaries, and anyone else dealing with family trusts, in those many moments of difficulty and frustration as well as the splendid moments of well-being. Nothing good or bad lasts.

For family trusts, there are many possible transition points:

- The trust's modification or "decanting" (explained below).
- The change of trustee.
- The change of beneficiary.
- The termination of a trust by the terms of the trust agreement.
- The termination of a trust by operation of law.

Sometimes these transitions are within the control of the interested parties. Sometimes they are not. But even in cases out of our control, we can plan for the possibility. There is another old saying: "Look to the end." Even if we cannot predict the end, and even if we will not be present at the end, thinking about the possible ends or outcomes can help guide our choices and actions today. For the one thing we know is that this too—the present state—shall pass.

Changing the Trust

Most family trusts are irrevocable, meaning that once established they cannot be changed significantly, especially when it comes to their distributive provisions. But as Solomon recognized, nothing on this earth is truly unchangeable, and a number of ways have arisen to make changes to supposedly irrevocable trusts.

We are not going to go in depth into these strategies. Their availability and form vary from state to state, depending on state law. The main strategies for making changes to irrevocable trusts include the following:

- Judicial settlement agreements.
- Judicial modifications.
- Decanting.

Judicial settlement agreements are perhaps the least burdensome way to change an irrevocable trust. In such an agreement, the trustee and all the beneficiaries—sometimes including representatives (usually appointed by the court) of minor beneficiaries—come together to agree to change the trust in some significant way. Such changes may include moving the distributive policy from an "income" distribution to a "unitrust" distribution (that is, a fixed percentage every year). Or the parties may agree to a particular interpretation of the distributive language around health or education or the like. Generally, a judicial settlement agreement cannot create or do away with beneficial interests, though such an agreement may be able to bring about the early termination of the trust. Again, state law and the circumstances dictate. As the name implies, a judicial settlement agreement must be blessed by a court, though it does not have to be prosecuted as a trial, which means it is much less expensive to obtain than a judicial modification.

A judicial modification or reformation, in contrast, requires filing a complaint and asking a court to investigate the request and render a decision. Before the advent of judicial settlement agreements, in many states this was the only way to make changes to an irrevocable trust. If such a process is required, the court will require all parties to be represented, including minor or unascertained beneficiaries. Depending on the complexity of situation and the court's docket, the process may also take a long time. Multiparty representation plus time equals significant lawyers' fees. Nor is a judge guaranteed to agree with whatever change the parties are asking for, even if all the adult parties have agreed to the change. After all, if the trust creator is dead and gone, the court may be very much inclined to leave matters in the form in which the trust creator created them—even if a change would seem to make all the sense in the world. The law is not known for its logic.

In the face of such constraints, trust attorneys and some states have in recent years devised a new strategy for changing supposedly unchangeable trusts: decanting. As the name implies, decanting involves "pouring" the assets of one trust into another. Usually, this pouring also involves moving the *situs* or the legal home of the trust from one state to another. This change may be desired because the new "home" allows for different treatment of the trust, such as not requiring as much notification of beneficiaries or more liberal delegation of trustee duties. In any event, decanting may allow for significant changes to the form of the trust, including the addition of a trust protector provision, changes to the administration of the trust, and division of trustee duties. Generally, it is not possible to make significant changes to beneficial interests. Decanting usually requires an agreement among trustees and beneficiaries and/or a court's blessing to move forward.

Whatever path one chooses in order to make changes to irrevocable trusts, it is crucial to involve all the stakeholders. A family trust by its nature lasts a long time, and people's opinions and attitudes may change over that time. Someone who was not properly informed of a change—even a positive one—years later may be offended or worse by being left out of the process. Given the possible expense and the possible disruptions to family relationships (not to mention the possible liability for the trustee), such changes should be approached with great care.

Changing the Players

Individual trustees and beneficiaries get old, sometimes become disabled, and always eventually die. Even institutional trustees may be swallowed up by other institutions; their personnel also retire or otherwise leave the scene.

What are thoughtful denizens of the trustscape to do in the face of these many possible changes? For trustees, we recommend that one of your primary duties is to prepare for your successor. This is a job that does not start when you are beginning to think of stepping down but rather when you first accept office. This preparation includes:

- Keeping clear and orderly records so that another trustee could, if need be, quickly come to understand the trust and the trustscape.
- Documenting your major decisions around administration, investments, and distributions so that a successor trustee could readily understand your thinking and your strategies.
- Encouraging the beneficiary to become a true partner in managing his or her trust, so that the beneficiary can apply those skills no matter who the trustee is.
- If you have the power to name your successor, keeping in mind possible candidates who could, at a moment's notice,

undertake the duties well and making sure that the beneficiary understands your power and is comfortable with your
possible successors.

- If the beneficiary has the power to name your replacement,
introducing the beneficiary to possible candidates for replacement and, when the time is right, guiding the beneficiary
through a process of interviewing, getting to know, and
selecting successor trustees.

- Ideally, serving side by side with a successor trustee so that
you can transition tasks and knowledge in a thoughtful
manner and help the beneficiary and new trustee go through
the process that we describe in earlier chapters for establishing
a firm and lasting relationship.

A beneficiary generally ceases to be a beneficiary only when
he or she dies or when the trust terminates.

Another way to manage long-term change in a trustscape is for
the trustee or a similarly responsible party to commission a 10-year
review of the trustscape. Such a process may include reviewing
who is serving as trustee and who are the primary beneficiaries;
which trusts are active and funded; how much they are paying out
or are planned to pay out in the next 10 years; which trusts are
likely to terminate in the next 10 years; how much the trusts are
costing in fees to investment advisers, trustees, and other parties;
what succession would look like should a current trustee die or be
forced to step down; what succession would look like should a
current beneficiary or even an entire class of beneficiaries pass
away; and where, to the best of anyone's ability to predict,
potential problem spots are. This review can be part of a larger
Family Trust Review, as we describe in Appendix 5.

When a trustee or beneficiary (and, one could add, trust
protector or trust adviser) leaves the trustscape, this transition
marks an important stage in the life of the trust and the system. As
such, it is important to give these transitions the benefit of ritual.

This ritual need not be complicated or involved. It may be something as simple as a celebratory dinner, a thank-you gift and letter of appreciation, or some sort of activity that embodies that proverbial "passing of the torch." As with any ritual (as we describe in *The Cycle of the Gift*), the elements here are threefold: first, a stepping back from the day-to-day business of life and the trustscape; second, a moment of reflection and learning and particularly appreciation and gratitude; and, third, a return to the everyday, armed with the learning and good feelings captured in the center of the ritual. Giving time and attention to such rituals is a key way to keeping the trustscape energized and alive through its long life.

Coming to an End

In the past, most trusts had a lifespan that was limited by the so-called "rule against perpetuities." Originating in the common law and incorporated into many statutes, this rule limits trusts to the duration of a "life in being" (e.g., the youngest living descendant of the current Queen of England) plus 21 years. The idea behind the rule seems to be that the "dead hand" of the trust creator should not be able to control property more than a 100 or so years after his or her own death. Life is for the living.

In recent years in the United States many states have greatly extended the rule against perpetuities (e.g., to 300 or even 1,000 years), while others have abolished altogether, allowing for the possibility of "perpetual trusts."[1] Nonetheless, many trusts still include some specification of their own termination. It may be that after the passing of the trust creator's own grandchildren, trust assets will flow to the great-grandchildren outright. It may be that after the trust assets have been divided below a certain size they will flow to their beneficiaries outright. Many trusts—such as charitable lead or remainder trusts—last for a specific term of years or for one person's life and then terminate, distributing their assets to their remainder beneficiaries.

Whether by operation of law (the rule against perpetuities) or by the operation of the trust agreement, it is crucial to attend to the ending of a trust, even if it is still years away. As we mentioned in Chapter 1, in a certain sense the highest duty of the trustee is to make sure that beneficiaries could, if need be, receive the trust assets and integrate them successfully into a healthy life. In the case of a terminating trust, this highest duty ceases to become hypothetical and may become very real. For an especially large and complex trust system, this situation is one in which an Office of the Beneficiary can be especially helpful. (For more on the Office of the Beneficiary, see Chapter 20.) This may also be a situation in which a Family Trust Review would be especially helpful (for a discussion of the Family Trust Review, please see Appendix 5).

In some cases, the termination of one trust leads—by the provision of the trust creator's will or by the estate plans of beneficiaries—to the creation of a new trust. In other cases, present beneficiaries who are receiving a terminating trust's assets may decide to give those assets to a new trust. In these cases, it is crucial to recognize that a new gift is taking place, and this new gift should receive all the consideration that any gift, from scratch, should receive: What is its purpose? What do the givers hope to achieve? Who are the recipients? How can they best integrate this gift into their lives? Does making this gift bring the givers joy? This is a perfect occasion for the new givers to create a preamble for their new trusts.

The termination of a trust also brings various duties for the trustee. The trustee must complete his or her accounting by sharing a full account of the trust's operations and final distributions with the present beneficiaries. Many trustees also ask the recipients to sign a release, after reviewing this final accounting, releasing the trustee from any further liability with regard to the trust. Such a release does not indemnify the trustee from past mistakes or malfeasance, but it does put a legal finality to the trustee's work.

Apart from such releases, as with the transition of trustees or beneficiaries, the termination of a trust also calls for a moment of ritual. That ritual could involve the present beneficiaries' gathering and reflecting on the impact that the trust has had on their lives. It could involve expressions of gratitude to the trust creator (who may be long gone) and the trustees, past and present. It may involve some discussion by the beneficiaries about where they plan to go from here, together or separately, and how the trust remainder will affect their plans. Sometimes trustees even compose a short history of the trust, to weave into the family's larger history.

Trusts may seem to be written in stone. But the only thing certain in life is change. We hope that these considerations about transitions help illuminate the many possible changes in even these seemingly unchangeable forms. Even more so, we hope that these thoughts prompt your own thinking about how to prepare for, manage, and even celebrate these transitions.

Note

1. For some thoughts about dangers inherent in perpetual trusts, please see Appendix 6.

Part Four

A COMPREHENSIVE MODEL FOR A HUMANE TRUSTSCAPE

Chapter 18

A Promise and a Challenge for Trust Creators

In the preceding chapters, we've taken you through a tour of the trustscape and its different roles and relationships. We've introduced those roles and defined them to varying degrees. We have also laid out specific practices for strengthening the relationships across the trustscape and for dealing with particular challenges around addictions, marriage, and transitions.

In the final part of this book, we want to move from this tour of structures and relationships that, in most cases, already exist, to a *prospective* journey into what could be. The practices and arrangements that we discuss in these final four chapters are being tested by a number of forward-thinking families. They are not yet widespread, but they are based on sound principles.

This vision of a humane trustscape is, we believe, best suited for trusts holding assets over $10 million. When the level is much lower, the envisioned structures might be too expensive and cumbersome. As the family's wealth approaches or exceeds $100 million or more, the family may want to consider a private trust company that in turn embodies these structures and functions within it or around it. (For more on private trust companies, see Appendix 4.)

Of course, whatever the range of a family's assets, our model of a humane trustscape is not going to be right for all trusts and all families under all circumstances. Please consider what you read in the following chapters as food for thought, to adapt and apply as best suits your family's or your clients' circumstances.

A Trust Creator's Challenge

Before beginning to paint this picture of a model trustscape in the next chapter, we first want to return for a moment to the fundamental challenge that trust creators face in selecting a trustee.

It's tempting to wish for a trustee who embodies the wisdom of Solomon, Buddha, and Nasrudin all rolled into one. If you know that person and he (or she) is available to serve your family—by all means, sign them up.

The closest you'll find to anyone who has pulled that off is an elderly Jewish grandfather who lived in New York City many years ago.[1] He scoured the country for just the right trustee for his grandson, who at that point was only eight years old and living in the Midwest. This grandfather's search ended when he met a 30-something Mormon attorney in Utah.

Following the grandfather's death, the trustee regularly visited the young man's mother (who was co-trustee). Each visit, this "friend of your grandfather's" spent time getting to know the beneficiary—long before the youth was told of the existence of his trust. This routine created the foundation for a lifelong relationship.

"The little things that my trustee as an adult did to reach out to me as a child were critical in the development of a rapport between the two of us," the beneficiary later reported. That beneficiary—today in his 50s—is grateful for the care his grandfather took in selecting a trustee who by now has been a mentor and friend for 40-plus years.

For the rest of us, the choice of a trustee usually comes down to a family member or maybe a friend, attorney, accountant, or professional trustee of one stripe or another (or some combination) who can adequately perform the trustee's three principal functions:

1. Performing administrative tasks like paying taxes and preparing statements.
2. Investing the trust's assets.
3. Distributing funds and generally relating to beneficiaries.

If a trustee needs a hand preparing a tax return? No problem—hire a certified public accountant (CPA). Lack investment expertise? There's a world of talented investment advisers ready to help.

But what if a trustee doesn't have the skill or interest that that young attorney had to relate well with beneficiaries?

We'll address that question and more.

First, an Exercise for Trust Creators

Before you meet with your attorney, your accountant, or your financial adviser to talk about trust structures, there's a weighty question for you to contemplate—one that's more important than any other trust-related question. For some of our readers, this will be your most difficult task when putting together an estate plan. Ask yourself: "Who are the people that I can count on to advocate for my trust's highest purpose, especially if that highest purpose is to promote the beneficiary's true freedom?"

A good place to start is to search your mental "my contacts" database for someone who's successfully navigated a really good midlife crisis. That's not to say someone much younger couldn't be just the right fit. Good judgment and compassion are what you're looking for. Think too about the principles that we shared in the Introduction, and the list of questions in Chapter 9 that a prospective trustee should ask.

But over the course of several days keep coming back to this question: who can you count on to advocate for your trust's highest purpose? Be on the lookout for candidates to fill a position that has this job description: someone having the wisdom, the strength, the compassion, and the time to take on the advocacy task.

Would it help to brainstorm with a family member, a friend, or a trusted professional adviser?

When you're ready, list the names that you come up with.

To some of our readers, thinking about people before thinking about documents, jurisdictions, and taxes will seem very different from what's usually expected or what's usually done.

Here's another surprise. The people that you listed are *not* necessarily candidates to fill the trustee's role. In fact, it may be wise to find places for such individuals in roles other than the trustee, and, for a trustee, to use an institution rather than an individual. What we have in mind for the trusted people on your list and why we think it may make sense to use an institutional trustee will become clear over the next three chapters, especially in Chapter 21.

Note

1. Adapted with permission from "My Grandfather's Gift," in *TrustWorthy*. © Trustscape LLC.

Chapter 19

The Highest Duty of the Trustee and the Corresponding Responsibility of the Beneficiary

To begin to paint the picture of a model trustscape, we'll start with another true story that shows how two wealth creators plus two advisers, times two years, can equal zero, at least temporarily.

The trust officer arrives at a modest house at around 9:30 A.M.—30 minutes before the meeting is scheduled to begin. He's greeted at the door by his hosts, a couple who own a ranch and are now well into their 80s. The wife escorts him into their "sitting room." The husband follows.

They wait for the attorney and certified public accountant (CPA) to arrive. The husband doesn't say much as his wife explains to the trust officer that they built this home many years ago. They raised their two sons here and never saw a reason to build a larger one.

Their attorney was the one who invited the trust officer to sit in on the meeting. During the past two years or so, this couple has met regularly with their attorney and CPA to design an estate plan. Husband and wife want the ranch to stay in the family and eventually go to their two sons, now in their 50s. The sons have helped to run the ranch since they were teenagers.

After two years of conversations about the estate plan, and multiple drafts of documents providing for trusts here and partnerships there, nothing has been signed.

The attorney knows that the trust officer has helped other couples mired in similar circumstances. Maybe he could help break this impasse.

The attorney and CPA arrive. The meeting will take place around the dining room table. As they walk from the sitting room to the dining room, the wife whispers to the trust officer, "I'm worried about my husband. He still spends as much time as he ever has at the ranch office. I've asked him to cut back. He's not as young as he used to be."

Here, we'll condense a conversation that played out at the dining room table.

"Your wife told me that you're at the office for a lot of hours."

"That's true."

"Is that because you're working as much as ever or because you like to hang out with your boys?"

"No, I'm working. I'm still running the ranch."

"What would happen if you were out of the picture? Could your sons run the ranch without you?"

"Well, neither could by himself. But together they could."

"They *could*, but *would* they?"

The husband tilts his head downward and closes his eyes for what seems like a very long time, although in reality it's probably fewer than 30 seconds.

"No, they wouldn't!" (Another pause.) "Here's what I want to do. It will take me about two years to wrap up a couple of deals that I'm working on. Then I want to sell the ranch, keep enough to support my wife and me, and split what's left between my sons. There will be plenty for each of them to buy their own ranch, if that's what they want to do."

I Wrote These Great Docs, but My Clients Won't Sign . . .

What's the most common complaint of attorneys who create estate plans? You can probably guess: "I wrote these great documents. Each is state of the art, protecting against taxes, creditors, and spendthrifts. But my clients won't sign them!"

If you're new to the world of trusts, that situation—and the authors have seen many like it—might seem ridiculous. How can all that professional time and talent be wrong? But perhaps you can empathize if you have ever tried to capture a complex business collaboration or even something like the construction of a new home into a binding legal document. There are the experts, offering wonderful documents, and then there's you, with your unique perspective and concerns.

The estate planning disconnect often begins with the questions that a family and its counsel bring with them to the planning process. Are the questions about preventing bad things from happening, driven by worry? About taxes? About creditors? About disputes? About second-rate trustees? If you go there, you get quickly stuck in the quagmire.

Or do the questions seek positive outcomes—in particular, a concern with enhancing the lives of beneficiaries? These families will spend the time necessary to understand the characteristics of a highly functional trustscape and will say: "I want that."

To get out of the mire and stay out, we recommend beginning by becoming familiar with the highest duty of the trustee and the corresponding responsibilities of the beneficiary in a trustscape that's working well. The model for a thoughtful trustscape then flows from these starting points.

The Highest Duty of the Trustee and the Corresponding Responsibility of the Beneficiary

In Chapter 1, we introduced an unconventional idea that may have left more than a few readers wondering what we meant:

> The *highest duty of a trustee* is to be able to say to the beneficiaries: "You could take this money tomorrow and you'd be fine if the trust were to end." And the corresponding responsibility of the beneficiary is to receive those funds well.

This bold statement is contrary to what is usually expected by trustees and beneficiaries. It's a "highest duty" that most people have never seen before.

Put another way, to be an able partner with their trustee, beneficiaries must be knowledgeable about the same three functions that the trustee must master.

1. Performing administrative tasks like paying taxes and preparing statements.
2. Investing the trust's assets.
3. Distributing funds and generally relating to beneficiaries.

Anything short of that and the relationship between trustee and beneficiary is at risk of becoming rigid and unresponsive, and of losing much of its ability to adapt. And unfortunately that's how most trustscapes operate. They look something like Figure 19.1.

In this simple depiction of the traditional trustscape, the co-trustees (an institution and an individual) are the center of the trustscape. They float above the beneficiary. The two trustees may or may not have a close and communicative relationship (an ambiguity represented by the dotted line). But they definitely rule over the beneficiary, with top-down communication (represented by the one-way arrow). In some trustscapes a trust protector hovers over the whole system, its function broad, vague, maybe even mysterious.

Is this a collaborative system? Definitely not. Collaboration can't exist when the two parties are not, at least for the most part,

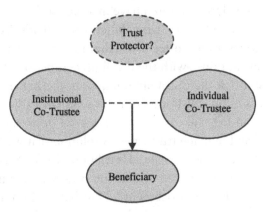

Figure 19.1   The Traditional Trustscape

on the same page about functions and end results. This point is decisive. There's no way around it.

So, if the trustee is to fulfill its highest duty, the question for the trustee becomes: If I'm not competent to perform one or more of the three functions, to whom do I turn?

And if the beneficiary is to fulfill his or her fundamental responsibility, he or she must ask, "Who will mentor me?"

These questions point to the pieces that are generally missing even in the most sophisticated trustscapes.

Support for the Trustee

As mentioned earlier, this book doesn't need to detail options for performing trust administration and investing. An individual who is serving as trustee will often retain attorneys and accountants to help with legal compliance, record keeping and preparing statements, preparing tax returns, and other administrative tasks.

That same trustee can also hire one or more advisers to help him make investment decisions. Of course, absent direction otherwise, responsibility for the decisions and their process (and liability if things go wrong) remains with the trustee.

Institutional trustees often have in-house staff to perform the administrative and investment functions. What's lacking are resources to assist the trustee—whether the trustee is an individual or an institution—with the distributive function. This is one more reason that the distributive function, the highest function of a trust, is often still-born from the moment of its creation.

What can help fill this gap and begin to bring about a truly thoughtful and humane trustscape? A solution that we have seen some families adopt is to create a Distribution Committee. Ideally, this is a committee created within the trust instrument, though even if not in the trust document a Distribution Committee can still be formed. The committee's sole responsibility is to advise the trustee about a beneficiary's requests for distribution. The committee is proactive, not reactive, because its members take time to know the beneficiary well. When a beneficiary is contemplating a request for funds, committee members will ask questions of the beneficiary to ascertain whether approving the distribution is in the beneficiary's best interest. Following their conversations with the beneficiary, committee members will enlighten the trustee.

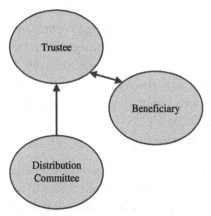

Figure 19.2   The Distribution Committee

As Figure 19.2 reveals, the Distribution Committee serves the trustee, not the beneficiary. But it allows the trustee to have a clearer and more collaborative relationship with the beneficiary, one that begins to move the beneficiary towards the center of the system and make their communication bidirectional rather than one-way.

It may be helpful for some readers to compare the Distribution Committee to the common institution of an investment committee. An investment committee relies on its knowledge of investing to advise the trustee about what to buy and sell, but it does not do the actual buying and selling. It's a means of helping the trustee fulfill his or her duty. The same would go for the Distribution Committee. It would not decide what to distribute or not. But it would develop knowledge about the beneficiary and use that knowledge to advise the trustee regarding this most important function.

Support for the Beneficiary

Some people would say that the trustee's job description includes mentoring beneficiaries. And for certain trustees, such as the young lawyer mentioned earlier, that's a welcome part of the job. However, there's no end of trustees who lack the skill, the interest, or the time required to mentor well.

For some families, the solution is to send their beneficiaries off to one or more "boot camps" to learn about investing and other technical topics.

Questions for reflection:

- What is gained and what is lost when a beneficiary attends a program that is excellent when it comes to teaching technical skills, but downplays relationships, self-awareness, and personal growth issues specific to beneficiaries?
- Who do I know who can help me learn about different programs that are available to educate beneficiaries?

Now imagine . . .

You are a teen or 20-something (and if you are a beneficiary reading this, you might very well be). Grandpa tells you about the three-day program for beneficiaries that he's enrolled you in this summer. He assures you that the time spent will be a great investment in your future. You will learn all about investing, budgeting, and a whole range of other financial survival skills.

Read between the lines and the message becomes: You will attend if you have any hope of receiving funds from your trust! For many beneficiaries, this message is all they can hear. And that's completely understandable.

What are the odds that you will show up but do little more than go through the motions for three days?

Now back to you, the reader. Over the years, you have no doubt enrolled in workshops, seminars, and maybe now and then a full course. Perhaps your profession requires "continuing education." Or maybe you signed up for personal growth reasons.

Now imagine that the program you attended was terrific—great material and a great presenter. You come away thinking about all the things that you can do with this new information. It all makes so much sense!

If you're like the authors (who have attended many a professional program over the years), here's what happens—and more often than we'd care to admit:

1. I leave the program all jazzed up.
2. A couple of weeks later, I remember the big ideas that I learned.
3. A month later, I remember that I really enjoyed the program. But remind me: what was it that I learned that was so compelling?
4. And three months later, I can't remember where I stashed the course materials.

Why would a beneficiary be any different?

A solution to this "business as usual" state of affairs is being pioneered by the authors and a small number of families. It is to establish a new entity called the Office of the Beneficiary (OTB). The sole purpose of the OTB is to assist the beneficiary to come up to speed in areas necessary to successfully address the question, "If my trust were to terminate tomorrow and the assets distributed to me, what would I need to know, and what skills would I need to master, to take that event in stride?" As Figure 19.3

shows, just as the Distribution Committee serves the trustee, so
the Office of the Beneficiary serves the beneficiary.

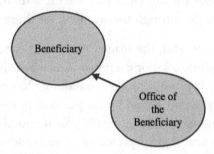

Figure 19.3   The Office of the Beneficiary

The OTB and the distribution committee are the two key
elements we see as forming the heart of a thoughtful trustscape.
We look at them more closely in the next chapter.

Chapter 20

The Distribution Committee and the Office of the Beneficiary

I n Chapter 19, we previewed the Distribution Committee (DC) and the Office of the Beneficiary (OTB). Since these two concepts are unfamiliar to most practitioners, not to mention trust creators and beneficiaries, they no doubt raise many questions in the minds of our readers. This chapter aims to shed more light on these groundbreaking innovations.

Distribution Committee

As we did in Chapter 19, let's first recall the comparison of this
new model with the traditional trustscape (Figure 20.1).

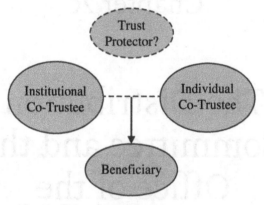

Figure 20.1   The Traditional Trustscape

In the traditional model the trustee or co-trustees form the
center of the trustscape and they give direction (including
approval or disapproval of distribution requests) to the beneficiary. The case starts to look quite different when a Distribution
Committee enters the scene (Figure 20.2).

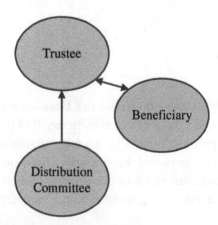

Figure 20.2   The Distribution Committee

The first impact of the DC is that the beneficiary starts moving to the center. After all, the DC's sole function is to fully understand the beneficiary, be familiar with the thinking behind his or her requests for funds, and advise the trustee accordingly.

This Committee should be made up of one or more individuals who have the wisdom to ask the kinds of questions that broaden a conversation. For example, "Can you tell me a little more about what this distribution, if it's approved, would do to enhance your life? How would it add to your human capital? If you didn't have access to this trust, how would you go about pursuing this same goal? What are your dreams, and how would this proposed distribution further them?"

A second characteristic common to DC members is the skill to listen deeply before responding. The DC does not start with a "yes" or a "no," but rather a, "Tell me more . . ."

Serving on the DC would be a great role for your most trusted adviser or a trusted friend, or for a family member who understands the conflict inherent in the dual roles of family member and committee member.

"Hold on," we hear an array of readers saying: "I thought that these very same qualities are ones that I'd be looking for in a trustee or a trust protector!"

Correct—within the traditional model. The reality is that a person having these characteristics often will decline to serve as trustee for any one of a number of reasons. Sometimes it's the time commitment. Sometimes it's a lack of knowledge or skills associated with performance of the trustee's responsibilities. Sometimes it's a concern with the potential liability faced by trustees.

Fiduciary liability for members of the DC should not be a problem if the trust instrument is properly drafted. (If the trust instrument does not mention the DC, and the trustee simply convenes a DC outside the trust to give him or her advice, then it is even less likely that the DC would have taken on a fiduciary role.) The DC does not have responsibility for making decisions. The final decision about distributions lies with the trustee. So, just as the investment committee advises the trustee on what to buy and sell—but does not actually buy and sell—the distribution function ultimately rests with the trustee.

This is a crucial point. The DC is not the decision maker. The authority to make distributions remains with the trustee. The DC is a resource for the trustee in order to fulfill that function, the distributive function, wisely and well.

In putting this model into practice, people often wonder about the relation between the DC and a trust protector. After all, a trust protector may also seek to get to know the beneficiary, understand his or her distribution requests, and talk such requests over with the trustee. However, while the qualities desired in a DC are very similar to the qualities that you might look for in a trust protector, the two roles are not easily combined. That is because in the model that we are advocating here, the trust protector will have a single, clearly defined judiciary role, which we will discuss at more length in the next chapter. Serving in this limited, judiciary role would be at odds with getting involved in the system in the way a DC must.

Because the DC concept will be new to many attorneys, and if it is to stand as part of the trust document, the trust creator may be the only one who can make sure the concept is on the table. In addition to what's already been mentioned, points to make clear in the trust instrument include:

- All costs associated with the DC are to be paid by the trust.
- Beneficiaries will not have authority to add members to, or remove members from, the DC. The DC serves trustees, not beneficiaries.
- The DC exists for the duration of the trust.

Of course, if an existing trust does not include the DC role, it is perhaps possible to use a settlement, reformation, decanting, or even a broadly empowered trust protector to add a DC to the trust instrument. (For more on making changes to existing trusts, recall Chapter 17.) Again, it is also possible that a trustee may want to convene a DC on his or her own initiative, just as a trustee may hire an investment adviser without having an "Investment Committee" role written into the trust. Of course, in such a case the trustee will have the power to do with (or without) a DC as he or she sees fit.

The DC can take a variety of forms. It may include several members with varying terms. It could start out as a committee of one. It could even be composed of officers from a company that the trustee hires because they possess the requisite psychological and trustscape knowledge, just as officers of an investment advisory company hired by the trustee may, in essence, serve as the investment committee. Whatever the exact form of the DC, the key is its function: to develop knowledge about the beneficiary that allows it to advise the trustee on making wise distributions from the trust, that is, distributions that truly help the beneficiary grow and become a free and flourishing individual.

The Office of the Beneficiary

Just as we did with the DC, let's remind ourselves of the basic look of the OTB (Figure 20.3).

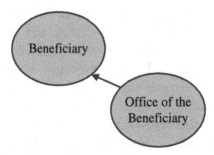

Figure 20.3   The Office of the Beneficiary

The principle of the OTB is this: beneficiaries should have their own office made up of people qualified to take them through a process of becoming excellent beneficiaries. By "excellent beneficiaries" we mean people who have developed the capacity to thrive even if their trust were to terminate and the funds be distributed on short notice; such beneficiaries could integrate that "meteor" without it throwing their lives off balance. (For more on excellent beneficiaries, recall the discussion in Chapter 7.) Another way to put this same point is this: because he or she is not dependent on trust distributions, an excellent beneficiary could thrive even if his or her trust were to disappear tomorrow, along with all its assets.

To that end, the OTB will mentor beneficiaries in the areas of trust administration, investing trust assets, and distributions. Just as importantly, the OTB will mentor beneficiaries in developing their capacities in such areas as work, relationships, and communication.

The OTB is not a college. As a mentor, it will expect that each beneficiary will be actively involved in developing his or her individual development program. No two such programs look alike.

For this same reason, every OTB is transitory in nature. It's deliberately designed to reduce the likelihood of morphing into an ongoing mechanism that creates dependency. It goes away when it's no longer needed.

Unlike the DC, the OTB is outside the trust. Beneficiaries have the responsibility to convene, staff, and decide when to disband an OTB. With that responsibility comes an economic obligation: costs are paid by the beneficiaries. Of course, if asked, a trustee might determine the costs to be a valid expense of the trust. But, ultimately, costs are to be borne by the beneficiaries.

A key principle here is that beneficiaries have financial "skin in the game." If a beneficiary believes an OTB will be useful, the proof is their willingness to pay for it.

The OTB is not some informal group of friends and discussants. Rather, it needs to be a formal relationship acknowledged by the trustee. So, for example, the trustee will provide the OTB with documents and reports. (To do so the trustee may need to have direction from the trust document or at least agreement by the beneficiary.) In that respect, it also differs from a beneficiary simply deciding to retain a mentor or two.

And unlike working with a mentor to improve one's golf swing or sharpen one's writing ability, the OTB will focus on three specific areas.

Trust Administration

The beneficiary will become familiar with the language of the trust agreement, the relevant law, and the trustee's policies and procedures. The beneficiary will understand the trust statements that are prepared by the trustee, which will require general knowledge of investments and trust accounting.

Rarely will a beneficiary want to spend time on matters of trust administration. So if the OTB reviews trust tax returns, reviews trust accountings, reviews the investment reports, reviews legal questions, confirms calculation of fees, and then reports to the beneficiary, the beneficiary is on the way to fulfilling the duty to understand trust administration.

Once the beneficiary has a good grasp of the administrative functions, he or she is likely to pass the day-to-day tasks to his CPA. At that time, this administrative function of the OTB will be discontinued.

Investment of Trust Assets

On the investment side, the beneficiary has a responsibility to understand strategic risk. The beneficiary will likely have continuing conversations with the OTB's trust investment expert addressing questions such as: What is the nature of the trust property? Is further education required about stocks, bonds, mutual funds, partnerships, investment real estate, closely held businesses, oil and gas interests, or other types of assets? What is the investment plan for the trust? Are the current investments consistent with the investment plan? Is there sufficient liquidity in the investment portfolio? The answers to these questions will require a general knowledge of modern portfolio theory, the prudent-investor rule, and trust accounting.

Once the beneficiary feels competent in this arena, the expert will no longer be needed.

Distributions from Trust

Here, the mentoring process is harder to define, so we'll take a more detailed look at some of the ground that may be covered.

The trust beneficiary will address the fact of his or her trust's existence and its implications for his or her life at increasing levels of understanding. He or she will move from assimilating fundamental information to successfully attending to relationships, to seeking personal well-being and fulfillment. As he or she integrates this learning, the beneficiary will reframe the trust. The trust will be seen less as a focal point of life and more as a resource to help him or her realize his or her potential, at whatever level that might be.

At the most concrete level, the task of the beneficiary will be to understand the roles and responsibilities of the beneficiary and the trustee, as well as the rules that govern the trust relationship.

At the next level of understanding, the beneficiary will recognize the trust to be a relationship among the trust creator, the trustee, the beneficiary, and perhaps other trustscapers. His or her task shifts from assimilating information to attending to these relationships well. He or she will become proficient at understanding, nurturing, and taking full advantage of the relationships.

At the highest level of understanding, the beneficiary will reach a new level of maturity with respect to the trust. He or she will view her trust as a gift of love, that is, as financial capital to be deployed in the service of her journey toward a fulfilling, productive, meaningful life. He or she will also be ready to integrate the trust into the major areas of life, including work, other relationships, and communications with friends and loved ones.

A beneficiary can't get to this point without asking some big questions: Have I reached a point in my life where I would like to live with more meaning and purpose? What would living my life with authenticity look like? What are my dreams, passions, and ambitions? What would I like to accomplish? Do I have a vision for the next phase of my life or beyond?

The important nuance here is that the focus is no longer just on the trust and its attendant relationships. The trust is properly positioned as a resource contributing to a satisfying life.

For most beneficiaries this journey of learning and personal development is not linear. The path may fold back upon itself. The trust beneficiary is likely to move in and out of the levels of understanding described above. Tasks related to the different levels will be undertaken simultaneously with varying degrees of overlap and varying degrees of success. The beneficiary will find it useful to be aware at any given time of the tasks in which he or she is engaged, where the tasks fit within the process, and where to seek assistance when needed.

To further this work, some OTBs use assessment tools to understand each beneficiary's learning and social styles. How much time can be saved (and frustration avoided!) if a beneficiary can learn how best he or she learns. Such assessments can also be crucial for helping a beneficiary think through what types of career or other work to pursue and to help beneficiaries begin to fit into the family's governance structure, if that is something desirable.

As the beneficiary successfully pursues and completes goals, he or she increases her confidence, gains life satisfaction, and builds momentum. He or she will come to understand that the journey is as important as the destination. He or she will be leading the life that he or she was meant to live.

Again, the OTB will not only teach the beneficiary about all these matters but will also guide the beneficiary through his or her own discovery as a mentor. This means that the personnel of the OTB may change over time. At one point the OTB may draw upon the expertise of lawyers or accountants who can teach and who can help the beneficiary discover the questions he or she really needs to ask. At other points the OTB may draw upon the skills and knowledge of personnel more skilled in the psychological aspects of exploring the trustscape, of planning a career, or of navigating relationships. A mentor-leader may be a constant in the OTB, remaining by the beneficiary's side and drawing others into the process as needed. As with the Distribution Committee, the OTB could also be staffed by officers of a company specifically devoted to doing this work with beneficiaries. The forms are many. The purpose—to guide the beneficiary towards a fuller understanding and a more flourishing life—remains the same.

In establishing an OTB, it may be tempting to treat it as a function of an established family office. The family office likely has employees who could educate beneficiaries in some of these areas, including trust administration and investments. The family office also has an interest in getting to know beneficiaries closely and helping them develop in healthy ways.

For the reasons mentioned earlier, we see it as crucial that beneficiaries feel "ownership" over "their" OTB, including paying for the OTB's work. Making the OTB part of the family office may make this sense of ownership impossible. That does not mean, however, that a beneficiary's OTB could not call upon resources from the family office to do its work. For example, why should the OTB have to hire an outside accountant or investment manager to help in a beneficiary's education in these areas if excellent professionals are available close to home? If the OTB does draw upon the family office's resources, the key is that the beneficiary feel that the OTB is working for him or her in marshaling those resources.

Conclusion

Here is what the model of a human trustscape begins to look like, with the DC and OTB both integrated (Figure 20.4).

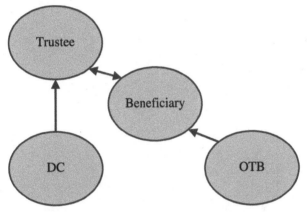

Figure 20.4   Model Trustscape with DC and OTB

The DC serves the trustee; the OTB serves the beneficiary. The trustee and the beneficiary have an open and trusting line of communication. The entire system puts the beneficiary at the center of things.

A particularly powerful combination that we have seen some families create involves using a DC and OTB in conjunction with a private trust company (PTC). To learn more about this combination of functions and PTCs more generally, please see Appendix 4.

As we mentioned, the DC and the OTB are relatively new developments that we have initiated with a few, far-seeing families. But the purposes that they meet are enduring. The creation of a DC or OTB is not for every trustscape and trustee. But our experience has been that many trustees welcome OTBs and DCs once the concept is understood. After all, beneficiaries who are understood and who show interest in their own development tend to work well with their trustees. Isn't that what a flourishing trustscape is all about?

Chapter 21

The Trustee and the Trust Protector Revisited

Whave now filled out some of the main parts of our picture of a truly humane trustscape. That picture begins with a trust creator who wants his or her trusts to fulfill the high purpose not of just stewarding financial assets but rather of developing great beneficiaries—that is, human beings who will flourish whether or not these assets are held in trust for them. From this intention flow not only the trust itself but also two critical institutions: a Distribution Committee (DC) that seeks to understand each beneficiary and to advise the trustee on distributions that will promote that beneficiary's growth, and an Office of the Beneficiary (OTB) that will work with each beneficiary to map out a path of personal learning and development, often supported by and in concert with the efforts of the trustee. This intention, embodied in these two institutions, can begin to create a truly humane trustscape (see Figure 21.1).

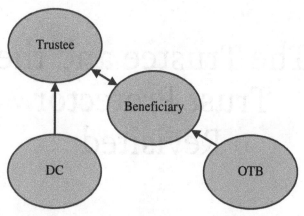

Figure 21.1   Initial Model of a Humane Trustscape

The model of a truly humane trustscape naturally brings with it changes to the role of the trustee and particularly of the trust protector. We reviewed the basics of these two roles in Chapters 6 and 8. What we want to share here does not contradict any of what we said there. Instead, it builds upon those points, to refine these roles and bring out their possibilities in this new model. Again, these innovations will not be for every trustee and every trust protector. But we have seen these changes play out with powerful, positive implications in several thoughtful trustscapes.

To begin to reconsider the roles of trustee and trust protector, recall for a moment the typical trust creator's stress as he or she confronts the question of who to name as trustee. "Do I ask a family member? A reliable adviser? A bank or other institutional trustee?"

The search can't go on forever. Once the search turns into a request of a particular person to serve, the anxiety generally becomes shared by that person: "Do I have the skill? The insight? The patience?" In the remainder of this chapter, we hope to share some thoughts that can focus the trust creator's search and narrow, if not eliminate, the potential trustee and trust protector's anxiety.

Which Cap's on Top?[1]

Imagine that all the people who are under consideration to be named trustee for your family's trusts are seated at a table—family members, friends, trusted advisers, representatives of various institutional trustees, and so forth.

Scattered on the table is a collection of baseball caps. Every cap displays a clearly visible label that describes an interpersonal relationship from the beneficiary's point of view. So one cap is marked "Mom." Another is labeled "Uncle." Other caps read "Dad's Business Partner" or "Mom's Closest Friend."

The final cap bears the caption "Trustee."

As the exercise begins, everyone seated at the table is asked to don—one on top of another—the different caps that describe their relationships to the beneficiary. Since every participant is potentially a trustee, each will wear a "Trustee" cap in addition to others. So Mom is wearing both a "Mom" cap and a "Trustee" cap. And Uncle Joe might have perched on his head an "Uncle" cap, another that says "Dad's Business Partner," and a third labeled "Trustee."

Recall the duty of fidelity described in the introduction to this book. That duty translates to this reality: at *all* times when someone is acting in the role of trustee, the Trustee cap must be placed on top of the all the others, taking precedence over all the caps that are piled up below it.

The question for each person seated at the table is: At those moments when I am acting in my role as trustee, can I temporarily keep in check all the other "caps" that I wear? Can I shift from "Mom relating to daughter" to "trustee relating to beneficiary"?

Similarly, under ordinary circumstances, Dad's adviser may defer to Dad's wishes, much as Mom's best friend will be loyal to Mom. But the moment that Dad's adviser, or Mom's best friend, puts on a "trustee" cap, that relationship must trump all potentially conflicting allegiances.

Can you see the inherent conflicts?

Recognizing these challenges leads to a question for trust creators: who among the trustee candidates will best be able to acknowledge, and then set aside, their conflicting roles?

It also leads to a question for potential trustees: will you be able to acknowledge, and then set aside, your conflicting roles while acting as trustee?

A Different Approach

Some families are finding success at the task of selecting trustees by trying a different approach: they decide upon a trust protector *before* selecting a trustee. By doing so, concerns and anxieties about the beneficiary's relationship with the trustee are immediately eased.

Here's how it works. The individual who was going to be trustee—the one who has maturity and practical wisdom, the one that you thought about back in Chapter 18—is instead asked to serve as trust protector.

This step may be a real attraction for the would-be trustee who is now asked to be trust protector. If structured properly, in most jurisdictions, the trust protector will not be considered a fiduciary. The practical effect is that some who might decline to be named trustee because he or she wouldn't want to take on potential liabilities that come with being a fiduciary, or because taking on a fiduciary role would create a conflict, can serve as a trust protector. For example, for liability reasons the family's legal counsel often removes him- or herself from the trustee selection process. Yet your lawyer may really know and like your family and want to help. Serving as trust protector might be the right solution.

In our model, this trust protector would have only one power, which lies dormant until it's invoked. This single power is to serve as the "judicial" branch of that particular trustscape if—and only if—the beneficiary (or perhaps the beneficiary or trustee) asks the protector to adjudicate a dispute.

During the time that his or her power lies dormant, the trust protector will take the initiative to get to know the trustee and the beneficiary. At least once a year, he or she will ask one, then the other: "How's it going?" The trust protector chats with the beneficiary. The protector chats with the trustee. He or she will not get involved in day-to-day trustscape affairs, merely staying informed. That way, in the event of a clash—unlike a judge who learns of a conflict only when it comes before the court—the trust protector will have the advantage of familiarity.

Now imagine that a conflict arises. Maybe the trustee denies a request for a distribution that, in the beneficiary's eyes, should be approved. The beneficiary says to the protector: "Look, I think the trustee made a decision without considering this and this and this. . . ."

The protector is in a position to say, "I'm not sure you're right about that, but I'll certainly look into it if you want me to. And by the way, what have you done, or not done, that has contributed to this state of affairs?"

This latter question is the fundamental question for the protector. It is designed to reduce blaming and spread awareness. It also creates an opportunity for learning. The trust protector's question prompts beneficiaries to learn and then be able to decide, "Do I really want to turn the trust protector's power on?"

Let's take this case one step further and imagine that the beneficiary reflects on the situation and decides that the trust protector should become formally involved. Once the protector's power is "turned on," his or her role is to attempt to mediate a solution that both trustee and beneficiary can live with. Failing that, the protector is all-powerful to remove the trustee and appoint a successor, or to retain the *status quo*.

In this model, the trust protector is purposefully given *only* a judicial authority. The trust protector is not deciding for or against a particular distribution or any other course of action. By living within these limits, the protector does not become a quasi-trustee. These limits are meant to mitigate against conflicts that may compromise the protector's ability to fulfill the judicial function objectively.

With the addition of this limited type of trust protector, the model now looks like this (Figure 21.2).

The beneficiary is now truly the center of the system. The dotted line between the beneficiary and the trust protector

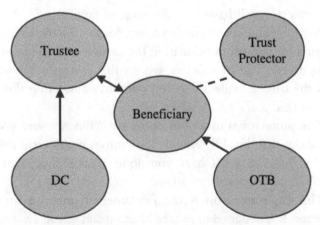

Figure 21.2   Model of a Humane Trustscape with Trust Protector

indicates the limited and largely dormant nature of the trust protector's role. If you want both the trustee and the beneficiary to have the power to "turn on" the trust protector, then you would have two dotted lines, one from the beneficiary to the trust protector and one from the trustee to the trust protector.

So, to return to the beginning, the person that the trust creator had in mind to serve as individual trustee has now been slotted to serve as the trust protector.

Now what? Who will be trustee?

Reconsidering the Institutional Trustee

"Why aren't institutional trustees used more often? Why is there a bias against institutional trustees?" Those two questions were posed to one of this guide's authors by a regional manager of a well-respected trust company. The manager was lamenting that institutional trustees are often selected by default, when more "desirable" candidates aren't available.

The response to the manager was that the problem institutional trustees have is that they are often seen as putting their own fees and risk management ahead of their loyalty to their clients.

The question of institutional loyalty is a real one. But what families don't realize is that it's almost impossible to find a layperson who has the interest and will take the time to learn all the things that go into being a good trustee: trust administration, investing, and proper distribution. And very few laypeople fully understand the duty of fidelity, the inherent conflicts of interest, and the potential liability if things go wrong. This is not to mention, as we did in Chapter 6, the advantages that institutional trustees bring in terms of solidity, endurance, and institutional memory.

An institutional trustee that leads with fidelity may be a good solution to addressing the administration and investment functions. But what about the function of getting to know the beneficiary well enough to fulfill the trustee's highest duty: preparing the beneficiary to receive assets well?

This is where we return, in our model, to the Distribution Committee and the Office of the Beneficiary. An institutional trustee, by itself, may find it difficult to get to know a beneficiary in the ways required to fulfill that highest duty of a trustee. The reality is that while institutions endure, institutional personnel often change, and the demands of present-day business many times preclude developing deep personal relationships with beneficiaries.

However, an institutional trustee that is informed by and working in concert with a DC and OTB is a completely different story. In this model, the institutional trustee can do what it often does best: maintain a sound and solid process of administration, investment, and distribution. As part of the latter process, it can rely on the insights of a DC. And it can outsource to the OTB the crucial work of helping the beneficiary develop. In fact, because they are so comfortable with process and with collaborative efforts, an institutional trustee may in many cases be the perfect trustee for partnering with a DC and OTB. The DC and the OTB bring deep and thoughtful attention to the human consequences of the trust relationships, while the institutional trustee provides a solid and enduring structure to the processes that surround those relationships (Figure 21.3).

This, then, is the outline of our vision of a humane trustscape: an institutional trustee working in harmony with a DC, an OTB, and a deeply trusted and wise trust protector. Viewed from the perspective of checks and balances, while the institutional trustee would have much of the formal power, that power would be informed by the DC and the OTB and, in the case of conflict, held in check by the trust protector. But life is more about flourishing than about checking and balancing power. The true virtue of this model is that it orients the entire system toward the

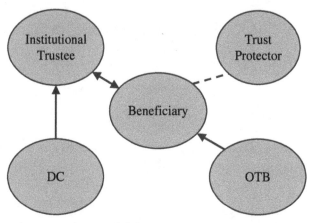

Figure 21.3   Complete Model for a Humane Trustscape

task of growing truly great beneficiaries. The institutional trustee provides the solid basis for this enterprise. The trust protector, though rarely active, keeps the focus on the long-term *human* impact of the system. And the DC and the OTB provide regularly updated information about and to the beneficiary as he or she charts life's journey.

It has taken a long time for the profession and for several far-seeing families to come to realize this humane vision. But now that it is coming to life, we, as practitioners and authors, hope for nothing more than that more and more families find a way to adopt this model. It has the potential to do untold good for generations to come.

Note

1. The authors thank Lee Hausner for teaching us a version of this exercise years ago.

APPENDICES

APPENDICES

Appendix 1

Sample Legacy Letter

The following multipart legacy letter is offered as an example meant to spur readers' thinking. Besides removing personally identifying information, we have not modified it, so its parts reflect the values and judgments of its authors. We do not mean to endorse these values or judgments. We have used this letter with gratitude to and the permission of its author.

LETTER TO TRUSTEES

Dear _____:

I. Purpose

I have spent a great deal of time thinking about how to arrange my estate after I die. I do this mostly because I want to give my family the best opportunity to thrive after me.

I do not wish for the money I leave behind to harm their pursuit of meaningful lives; rather, I would like it to be helpful.

My plans provide for trusts to benefit [WIFE] and [CHILD]. They call for you, [NAMES OF TRUSTEES] to serve as trustees. The relationships I am creating among you, on paper, will end up being incredibly significant in each of your lives. My sincere hope is that your relations will be positive, generative, and healthy.

I write this letter for the following purposes:

1. To help you understand what my hopes are for your relationships now and in the future.
2. To encourage you, now, to deepen your relationships with [CHILD] and [WIFE]. It is important that you know them well, and they you.
3. To inspire meaningful conversation between and among you, and me, about the principles that I wish to govern the discretionary decisions the trustees will be asked to make about money in the future.

What follows is meant to give you some things to talk about together and with me. It is not meant to go on your shelves or e-mail inboxes, collecting dust until my death. Let's get together and talk.

With that in mind, the rest of this letter and its enclosures are things I want you to know. Included are personal notes to [WIFE] and to [CHILD]. I have chosen to let you trustees "listen in" on these letters because I think it is important for you to know my feelings as you deepen your relationships with them now and in the future.

II. Exhibits

1. Ethical Will
2. Fiduciaries and Advisers Contact Info
3. Funeral Arrangement Letter
4. Statement of Financial Position

5. Estate Plan Diagram
6. Financial Planning Documents
7. Charitable Giving History
8. Investment Policy Statement

III. Ethical Will

I have included a copy of the current draft of my Ethical Will as Exhibit A. My Ethical Will describes many of my core values and life principles, including about life and money. Please read it carefully.

IV. Instructions at Death

Upon my death, *to the extent not already handled in my lifetime*, I would like you to consider these instructions:

1. My desire is to close my business. A diminishing number of executives and staff will need to remain as employees during this wind down and dissolution stage, as I expect for the business to collect on receivables and distribute the liquid assets to my estate. I am presently working on the sale of my business.
2. I have included a letter to [FUNERAL DIRECTOR] with instructions regarding my wishes for my funeral, attached as Exhibit C. My desire is to have a simple ceremony with nice music and a celebratory mood.

[Exhibit V, Messages to Wife, omitted.]

VI. Messages to [CHILD]

Dear [CHILD],

I am writing this letter to you to tell you what my hopes are for how you will benefit the most from the funds that I am leaving in trust for you. Being a young person with funds set aside for them is a big responsibility. I want it to help you find a meaningful life. I do not want it to hurt you.

While I am alive, I am responsible for deciding about your education and money. When I am gone, the trustees will perform this role.

There are five things I want to emphasize for you to help you on this path:

1. *Forge a meaningful relationship with your trustees.* I have some dear friends who have agreed to serve as your trustees. This is a major responsibility. They will have discretion to decide when and how to help you financially. I want your relationship with them to be close and meaningful. You have a responsibility to seek them out, to know them, to let them in on your life—your plans, hopes, dreams, and fears. Do this as early and often as possible. They have a responsibility to listen to you, care about you, and mentor you. They also have a responsibility to consider the values I have asked them to consider. Please give them your respect and understand that they have an important and challenging job to perform for you.

2. *Learn to be money wise.* I will have left you money in trust. Do not let it get in the way of your happiness. Too many people with money think they do not need to work, do not need to struggle, do not need to worry about understanding money, spending, budgets, and the like. Do not be that person. Learn about money. Learn about business and budgets and banks and investing. Learn how to read a bank statement, a financial statement, an investment report. Become a saver. Become a giver.

3. *Pursue education and learning.* Get an education. You are bright and curious. In the modern world, a young person like you should pursue a graduate-level degree. Beyond that, love to learn in all its forms, particularly through experiential world travel. The trustees should help you fund these pursuits.

4. *Work and contribute.* Find a meaningful vocation that allows you to use your incredible gifts to their fullest. It matters far less to me that this be financially rewarding, or how society perceives its values, and far more that you find meaning and fulfillment from it. Do not ever allow yourself to be lazy or dependent on others. Give of your own money and your time; we have a responsibility to help those less fortunate. Find some way to do this working together with others.

5. *Deal with conflicts.* There will be times when your trustees will have to make some really tough decisions. Sometimes those decisions will involve balancing what might be good for you with what might be good for your mother. Other times it might mean balancing what they think is good for you and your mother with what their bank co-trustee is doing with investing. Other times it might mean balancing what they want to do for you with what the law or my trust document says. Please be understanding and forgiving. They have a hugely challenging job.

I love you. I am proud of you. My time with you has been, and is, my greatest joy. I know you will flourish.

Your loving father.

VII. Messages to Trustees

Dear [NAMES OF TRUSTEES],

More than anything else, my message to you is this: get to know [WIFE] and [CHILD]; know them now, and forge a close relationship for the years to come. Be their friends and mentors. The rest of what follows is secondary to this grand hope. If you are close, I am confident that the rest will follow.

Beyond that, here are some additional thoughts I wish to share with you to help guide you with the many discretionary decisions you will need to make as my trustees:

First the obvious—follow the instructions in the trust agreements. My overriding intent about distributions is that the beneficiaries have financial peace and security, not superfluous excess. Be conservative with the investments of the trusts and maintain a long-term perspective. I have included for you the Investment Policy Statement that was developed with [INVESTMENT ADVISER] to monitor and assist in the investment guidelines that the corporate trustee should follow as managers of the estate. I shall talk further with you as to the function of each trust so that individual investment policy statements are developed for each trust.

The primary purpose of my trust during my lifetime with [WIFE] is to support our lives. After I am gone, it will be to support [WIFE]'s life. Any remainder will go to [CHILD]'s trust, where I would like it to support her care and education but preserve assets for educating her descendants.

My trust documents call for three individual trustees at all times, four while [WIFE] is alive. Individual trustees should retire at the earlier of incapacity or upon reaching the age of 75 years old. A trustee may voluntarily relieve him/herself of the responsibility as well.

You will have an appointed corporate trustee to do the "heavy lifting" for you: investing of assets, legal compliance/issues, income tax compliance, mitigating risk, and safeguard assets from creditors. Your primary focus will be to maintain relationships with the beneficiaries and to make discretionary decisions about the distributions from the trusts. A general summary of the estate plan is included as Exhibit E. I encourage you to cultivate good relationships with [LAWYER] and [TAX ADVISER], but you should feel no obligation to continue working specifically with them.

I have calculated the numbers and have included for you my most current statement of financial position (Exhibit D), family budget and capital need analysis (Exhibit F), and charitable contribution history (Exhibit G). You will see that based on the assumptions in these exhibits, if I die at 85 years old and then

[WIFE] at 85 years old, there should be $_____ million of investment assets, plus homes remaining at [WIFE]'s death. This is all calculated at a (hopefully) conservative long-term annualized investment return of inflation plus _____ percent.

Regarding distributions from trusts to beneficiaries:

All trustees must make decisions on distributions to beneficiaries, and I encourage you to maintain good communication with the corporate trustee. My overriding hope is that the trust funds we have provided for the beneficiaries will be used to enhance their lives and will not serve as an impediment to their happiness or sense of accomplishment and self-worth.

Be wise and discerning with distributions:

1. Do not enable long-term dependency on the funds that are distributed. I want them to be productive people who have a fully developed sense of self. If someone chooses a career that is a low-paying job, it is okay to underwrite them and support them with financial distributions.
2. Be aware of any possible substance abuse and avoid funding destructive behavior of this sort. Pay for rehabilitation services and promote reconciliation and recovery.
3. Be generous for educational expenses and to cover medical care costs.
4. Be supportive of international travel. There is so much to learn in the world outside of our daily lives.
5. Support entrepreneurial endeavors, but be wise in mitigating risks and require provision of a business plan to the Trustees with a request of funds.
6. Consider distributions for the purchase of a primary personal residence.

My desire is for [CHILD] and any children she may have to be educated in financial matters and be mentally engaged in the operations of her/their trust(s). The goal is for her to make informed financial decisions, so as not to purchase more shoes or frivolously spend money. I would like [CHILD] to work for things. Do not distribute large amounts of money without supportive reasoning. If she wants money for an entrepreneurial venture or investment, encourage her to have a material involvement in it.

I have a donor advised fund at [INSTITUTION] and would like for it to be divided into two separate donor advised funds upon my death. [NAMED PEOPLE] will be the successors of one DAF and will distribute those funds at their discretion to charitable organizations. The other DAF will have [NAMED PEOPLE] named successors and will have discretion of the distributions for the same purposes.

VIII. Reflections and Encouragement

If there weren't money involved, I would not be asking you to form relationships. Even though money is the reason I am asking you to build a relationship, my encouragement is that your relationships *not focus on money, but on what really matters in life*. Do this as part of your larger plans for building meaningful lives. Then I will look down and smile.

Now, let the conversations begin. You cannot know how much I look forward to sitting with each of you to talk.

All the best,
[SIGNATURE]

Appendix 2

Sample Language Regarding Addiction

Model Language for Family Governance Documents for Substance Use Disorders and/or Mental Health Concerns, from William Messinger, *The Trustee's Handbook for Addressing Addiction in Beneficiaries* (all rights reserved, used with permission).

Suggested Language Restricting Access to Principal and Income When a Beneficiary or Family Member May Have Problems with Alcohol, Drugs, Other Behaviors, and Activities or Mental Health Concerns

Trustee Authority Regarding Substance Use Disorders, Other Disorders, and Mental Health Concerns in a Beneficiary

1. Sole Discretion of Trustee to Withhold Income or Principal, Notwithstanding Any Other Provision of This Trust Agreement

a. Notwithstanding the foregoing as to distributions of income and principal, the Trustee in his/her sole discretion, shall withhold distributions of principal, income, or other withdrawals from any Beneficiary who has or may have: a substance use disorder(s), (addiction), other disorders, compulsive or destructive behaviors, mental health conditions or concerns, or any combination of the foregoing, as defined in paragraph 9, below.

b. Such principal, income, or specified withdrawals shall be retained and held by the Trustee until such time as the Trustee determines, in his or her sole discretion, that the Beneficiary is in recovery (as defined below in paragraph 6) from a substance use disorder(s), (addictions), other disorders, compulsive or destructive behaviors, mental health conditions or concerns or any combination of the foregoing, as defined in paragraph 9, below. Any amounts so withheld and accumulated may be retained in the Trust rather than distributed, at the Trustee's sole discretion. However, the Trustee is authorized to expend income and principal for the purposes set forth in this appendix.

c. If the Beneficiary dies before mandatory distributions or rights of withdrawal are resumed, the remaining balance of the mandatory distributions that were suspended will be distributed to the alternate beneficiaries of the Beneficiary's share as provided herein.

d. While mandatory distributions are suspended, the trust will be administered as a discretionary trust to provide for the Beneficiary according to the provisions of the trust providing for discretionary distributions in the Independent Trustee's sole and absolute discretion and as mandated by the appendix.

2. Authorization to Hire and Rely on Professional Expertise to Implement This Appendix

    a. The Trustee is authorized to employ and retain experts on: substance use disorder (addictions), other disorders, compulsive or destructive behaviors, mental health conditions or concerns, and resultant family conflict or any combination of the foregoing, as defined in paragraph 9 below, to advise him/her regarding any matters, issues, or determinations in this appendix. The Trustee may designate such experts to receive information or perform tasks on his/her behalf in order to implement this appendix.

        Further, the Trustee may employ experts to recommend comprehensive treatment and posttreatment recovery programs (meeting the standards in subparagraphs b and c below) and to oversee and implement such programs. The Trustee is also authorized to use the recovery programs for addicted pilots and physicians as part of an oversight program for the Beneficiary (or similar programs in the event the pilot or physician program is unavailable).

        In addition, the Trustee is authorized to employ and be advised by experts regarding entering into and preparing agreements (Recovery Contracts) between the Beneficiary and Trustee specifying recovery activities by the Beneficiary, including such activities that are funded directly or indirectly by the trust.

    b. The Trustee is further authorized to utilize and rely on the professional judgment of a reputable treatment center, utilizing an abstinence-based chemical dependency treatment model and recognized by the Joint Commission on Accreditation of Health Care Organizations, for evaluations, recommendations, and treatment regarding the Beneficiary's suspected or actual substance use disorders (alcohol/drug dependence and abuse). The

Trustee is similarly authorized regarding any other disorders, compulsive or destructive behaviors, mental health conditions or concerns or any combination of the foregoing, as defined in paragraph 9 below.

c. The Trustee has sole discretion regarding the employ and use of any such treatment centers or other resources such as supervised living facilities, halfway houses, sober homes, and wilderness programs as needed; however, all such resources shall be licensed or credentialed as per applicable state guidelines and standards described in the preceding paragraph. Any experts utilized by the trustee shall be licensed and credential as per applicable state standards and guidelines, with any professional authorized to prescribe medications certified by ASAM (Society of Addiction Medicine) or under the direct supervision and direction of an ASAM certified professional.

3. Authorization Regarding the Expenditure of Funds for Intervention, Treatment, and Recovery Activities

The Trustee has full authority and discretion to expend funds for advice regarding implementation of this appendix, to develop and implement plans for intervention in the event the Beneficiary may have a substance use disorder (dependent on or abusing alcohol or drugs) or may be actively using alcohol or drugs after treatment (relapse). Such authority includes expending funds for evaluations, treatment and all related costs, for posttreatment recovery programs, and any and all related matters deemed appropriate by the Trustee in his/her sole discretion. This paragraph (3) is fully applicable to other disorders, compulsive or destructive behaviors, mental health conditions or concerns, or any combination of the foregoing, as defined in paragraph 9 below, including noncompliant behavior with treatment plans and behavioral relapses.

4. Authorization to Receive Reports/Beneficiary's Consent to Release Information

   a. In making determinations as to whether the Beneficiary is participating in, has successfully completed an approved and applicable treatment program and/or is engaged in an active recovery program, the Trustee (and/or her/his designee) is authorized to receive reports from counselors and staff from treatment programs of any kind, sponsors, and all health care professionals or others providing assistance to the Beneficiary.

   b. In addition, the Beneficiary must fully comply with all recommendations of treatment programs and health care professionals, as approved by the Trustee (and/or his/her designee. The Beneficiary must sign consents for full release of information to the Trustee (and/or his/her designee) in order to be in compliance with this paragraph (4). Failure to sign all requested authorizations means the Beneficiary is not in "recovery" as that term is used in paragraph 6.

5. Alcohol and Drug Testing

   a. The Trustee (and/or her/his designee) shall utilize the services of a reliable and licensed drug testing company to randomly drug test the Beneficiary during the first two years of recovery (as defined in paragraph 6 above), and/or if the Beneficiary may be disputing whether he/she is using alcohol or drugs. The Trustee (and her/his designee) is authorized to require continued drug testing for as long as the Trustee deems such testing to be advisable, regardless of any other provision in this appendix. Full disclosure of results from such tests shall be made in a timely manner to the Trustee (and/or her/his designee).

   b. Such tests must be conducted under the observation of personnel from the drug testing service or their designee, and may include but not be limited to laboratory tests of hair, tissue, or bodily fluids. The physician in charge of the Physician's Health Program is the preferred resource for such testing.

c. The Trustee, in the exercise of sole and absolute discretion, may totally or partially suspend all distributions otherwise required or permitted to be made to the Beneficiary until the Beneficiary consents to the examination and complies with full disclosure of the results to the Trustee.

6. **Recovery—Two-Year Minimum**

a. **Recovery,** as used herein, is defined as no less than a minimum of two years of continuous sobriety (including abstention from narcotic prescription medicine, drugs, alcohol, or other addictive or compulsive behaviors or use disorders) and/or two years' continuous adherence to treatment plans in the case of mental health conditions. Only medications prescribed and approved by ASAM certified prescribers and consistent with the Beneficiary's **Recovery Program** will be considered as meeting the foregoing definition.

The definition of **Recovery** also includes, but is not limited to, ongoing participation in a **Recovery Program,** as determined by the Trustee or his designee: Activities addressing issues relating to substance use disorders (addiction), other disorders, compulsive or destructive behaviors, mental health conditions or concerns, or any combination of the foregoing, as defined in paragraph 9 below. (Examples: attending 12-step or other self-help groups, therapy, case management meetings; avoiding high-risk relapse environments; and adhering to recovery plans, recommendations, or agreements).

b. The two-year minimum shall be extended if the Beneficiary has a history of relapse, is not compliant with treatment plans, or fails to actively engaged in a recovery program, with such time extension(s) determined at the sole discretion of the Trustee.

c. In the event the Beneficiary has not completed the two-year minimum of recovery or extensions thereof, the Trustee has the discretion to disburse income and/or principal on behalf of the Beneficiary in amounts to support the Beneficiary's recovery program. Conversely, the Trustee shall not disburse funds for activities that might lead to relapse. The Trustee is authorized to rely on the advice of experts in implementing this Section 6 and otherwise exercising discretion as permitted in this appendix.

7. Date When Recovery Begins

The commencement of any time period of recovery begins after the Beneficiary has successfully completed chemical dependency inpatient primary treatment (or other addiction or mental health–related treatment) and any subsequent long-term, halfway, sober house, or wilderness program. (Such time does not commence upon entering treatment, but when successfully completing outpatient treatment or leaving a supervised or otherwise restrictive environment.) Successful completion of any such program is determined by the treatment provider and as approved by the trustee, who may rely on the advice and opinion or experts independent of any treatment center.

8. Distribution to Spouse, Children, or Other Family Members

In the event of withholding of or restriction on distributions to the Beneficiary, the Trustee is authorized to make distributions for the benefit of the Beneficiary, including those owed a duty of support by the Beneficiary, such as the Beneficiary's spouse, ex-spouse, children, or other family members.

The Trustee is authorized to make arrangements for the support of such individuals through distributions by alternative means, as the Trustee determines in his/her sole discretion, with the intent to maintain such individuals' lifestyle, including paying support staff and third-party vendors.

In the event any such individual meets the definition in paragraph 9, the trustee is authorized to provide services as set forth in this appendix herein. In the event any such individuals are in need of therapy, treatment or other forms of assistance due to the conduct of a Beneficiary meeting the definition in paragraph 9, the Trustee is authorized to provide services as set forth in this appendix.

9. Definition of Substance Use Disorder or Abuse and Other Addictions/Disorders

The phrase "Beneficiary who has or may have a *substance use disorder* (formerly dependent on and/or abusing drugs or alcohol), other disorders, compulsive or destructive behaviors, mental health conditions or concerns (including mental illness and mental disorders) or any combination of the foregoing," shall have meaning as defined in the DSM-V-TR (*Diagnostic and Statistical Manual of Mental Disorders*). The DSM-V criteria for "Alcohol Use Disorder" are at the end of this appendix. These definitions may be revised to reflect new medical information and/or credible research by recognized professionals, as defined in paragraph 2.

10. Indemnifications, Exoneration Provision, and Dual Capacity
   a. The Trustee (and any professional, adviser, assistant, or other person including their business entities, hired and/or retained by the Trustees) will be indemnified from the Trust Estate for any liability in exercising the Trustee's judgment and authority in this appendix, including any failure to request a Beneficiary to submit to medical examination and including a decision to distribute suspended amounts to a Beneficiary. This indemnification clause includes any allegations of any kind brought by the

Beneficiary, or on behalf of the Beneficiary, directly or indirectly against the Trustee and those hired and/or retained by the Trustee. If such allegations occur, the respondent has the option of requesting the trust to provide the defense or asking the trust to pay to the respondent funds for his/her defense.

b. It is not the Grantor's intention to make the Trustee (or any professional, adviser, assistant, or other person including their business entities, hired and/or retained by the Trustees) responsible or liable to anyone for a Beneficiary's actions or welfare.

c. The Trustee has no duty to inquire whether a Beneficiary uses drugs or other substance, but is expected to initiate the process specified in this appendix if circumstantial or direct evidence comes to the Trustee's attention that the Beneficiary is engaging in conduct specified in paragraph 1, to wit: the Beneficiary has a substance use disorder or may have other use disorders (addictions), compulsive or destructive behaviors, other disorders or mental health concerns or any combination of the above mentioned disorders, as defined above in paragraph 9.

d. A Trustee acting in the dual capacity as Trustee and family member is authorized to discuss with the Beneficiary and the Beneficiary's relatives, information the family member obtains in his capacity as Trustee, for the purpose of furthering the welfare of the Beneficiary.

11. Other Prohibitions during Withholding of Distributions

a. If distributions to a Beneficiary are suspended or withheld as provided above in this appendix, then the Beneficiary shall automatically be disqualified from serving, and if applicable, shall immediately cease serving, as a Trustee, Trust Protector, or in any other capacity in which the Beneficiary would serve as, or participate in, the removal or appointment of any Trustee or Trust Protector hereunder.

b. The withholding or suspension of benefits to the Beneficiary is sufficient evidence to suspend or terminate the Beneficiary's role in other family positions or activities. If the Beneficiary contests such suspension or termination, the Trustee is authorized to release information relating to the Beneficiary's addiction to the appropriate family governing body or authority.

(This language can be modified for use in business, succession, management, real estate ownership, family office, and philanthropy governing documents.)

Trust Protector Provision: It is advised to use a Trust Protector to permit this appendix to be modified due to changes in addiction treatment or as other conditions warrant.

Alcohol Use Disorder DSM-V

As defined in the *Diagnostic and Statistical Manual of Mental Disorders,* Fifth Edition (DSM 5, p. 490)

Diagnostic Criteria

A problematic pattern of alcohol use leading to clinically significant impairment or distress, as manifested by at least two of the following, occurring within a 12-month period:

1. Alcohol is often taken in larger amounts or over a longer period than was intended.
2. There is a persistent desire or unsuccessful efforts to cut down or control alcohol use.
3. A great deal of time is spent in activities necessary to obtain alcohol, use alcohol, or recover from its effects.
4. Craving, or a strong desire or urge to use alcohol.
5. Recurrent alcohol use resulting in a failure to fulfill major role obligations at work, school, or home.

6. Continued alcohol use despite having persistent or recurrent social or interpersonal problems caused or exacerbated by the effects of alcohol.
7. Important social, occupational, or recreational activities are given up or reduced because of alcohol use.
8. Recurrent alcohol use in situations in which it is physically hazardous.
9. Alcohol use is continued despite knowledge of having a persistent or recurrent physical or psychological problem that is likely to have been caused or exacerbated by alcohol.
10. Tolerance, as defined by either of the following:
    a. A need for markedly increased amounts of alcohol to achieve intoxication or desired effect.
    b. A markedly diminished effect with continued use of the same amount of alcohol.
11. Withdrawal, as manifested by either of the following:
    a. The characteristic withdrawal syndrome for alcohol (refer to Criteria A and B of the criteria set for alcohol withdrawal, pp. 499-500).
    b. Alcohol (or a closely related substance, such as a benzodiazepine) is taken to relieve or avoid withdrawal symptoms.

Specify if:

In early remission: After full criteria for alcohol use disorder were previously met, none of the criteria for alcohol use disorder have been met for at least 3 months but for less than 12 months (with the exception that Criterion A4, "Craving, or a strong desire or urge to use alcohol," may be met).

In sustained remission: After full criteria for alcohol use disorder were previously met, none of the criteria for alcohol use disorder have been met at any time during a period of 12 months or longer (with the exception that Criterion A4, "Craving, or a strong desire or urge to use alcohol," may be met).

Specify if:

In a controlled environment: This additional specifier is used if the individual is an environment where access to alcohol is restricted.

Specify if:

305.00 (F10.10) Mild: Presence of 2–3 symptoms.
303.90 (F10.20) Moderate: Presence of 4–5 symptoms.
303.90 (F10.20) Severe: Presence of 6 or more symptoms.

Because the first **12 months** following a Substance Use determination is a time of particularly high risk for relapse, this period is designated "Early Remission."

Appendix 3

The Distribution Committee

O ne of the most important new ideas presented in this book is that of the Distribution Committee (DC). Because of its novelty and significance, we have included this appendix to discuss in greater depth key elements of the concept and offer drafting points for new or existing trusts.

More than any single element of the trustscape, the DC ties together the major themes found throughout this book:

- The single most important reason for creating a trust is to make a gift of love that promotes the beneficiary's true freedom.
- Given this purpose, it follows that the highest duty of the trustee is to help prepare the beneficiary such that if the trust should end and the assets be distributed to the beneficiary tomorrow, the beneficiary will have the knowledge, the

maturity, and the competency to receive and steward the funds well.

- The practical question becomes: how can the trustee and other responsible parties ensure that this trust, and the relationships created or altered by this trust, enhance the beneficiary's life?

The Core Concept

As we discussed in Chapters 19 and 20, the purpose of the DC is to augment the distributive function so that (one hopes) the trustscape accomplishes its ultimate goal: to enhance the lives of the beneficiaries.

The DC's sole responsibility is to advise the trustee regarding a beneficiary's requests for distribution. To fulfill this responsibility, the members of the Committee must be proactive. That is, they will take time to get to know each beneficiary well in advance of a particular request for funds. This is contrary to the reactive posture of many trustees. ("I begin to consider a request when it lands on my desk.")

When a beneficiary is contemplating a request for funds, Committee members will seek to understand the context and underlying reasons for the request. The conversation may be brief or unfold over time, according to the complexity of the issues at hand. Depending on the needs of the beneficiary, this may present an opportunity for mentoring. In Chapters 13 and 14, we offered ideas for structuring productive conversations.

The Committee member's goal is (1) to help the beneficiary clarify his or her thinking and (2) to form an opinion as to whether approving the distribution would enhance the beneficiary's life in some manner. We discussed the meaning of "enhance" in Chapter 14. It's worth reemphasizing that the trustee's view of enhancing will change according to the beneficiary's stage of life.

In forming their opinion about a given distribution request, we urge committee members to be cognizant of their own "narratives" that may be influencing their analysis. Above all else, be open, honest, and transparent with beneficiaries.

Following their conversations with the beneficiary, committee members will enlighten the trustee about the beneficiary's thinking and make a recommendation.

It's important to note that the DC's duty is to the trustee, not the beneficiary. In this respect, the DC is analogous to an Investment Committee. An Investment Committee relies on its knowledge of investing to advise the trustee about what to buy and sell, but does not do the actual buying and selling. It's a means of helping the trustee fulfill his or her duty. The same goes for the DC. It does not approve or deny particular requests for distributions. That authority remains with the trustee. The DC develops knowledge about the beneficiary and uses that knowledge to advise the trustee regarding this most important function.

Committee Members

The key criterion for membership on a DC is not technical knowledge of trusts, though certainly such knowledge can help in the background. Instead, the DC should be made up of one or more individuals who have the wisdom to ask the kinds of questions that broaden a conversation. These are questions designed to lead to creative perspectives and either convergent or divergent thinking, as appropriate.

A second characteristic that should be common to DC members is the skill to listen deeply before responding.

A third characteristic is self-awareness and emotional intelligence.

Serving on the DC would be a great role for your most trusted adviser or a trusted friend, or for a family member who understands the conflict inherent in the dual roles of family member and committee member.

These same qualities may look, to many readers, as the ideal qualities for an individual trustee. But the reality is that a person having these characteristics often will decline to serve as trustee for any one of a number of reasons. Sometimes it's the time commitment. Sometimes it's a lack of knowledge or skills associated with performance of the trustee's responsibilities. Sometimes it's a concern with the potential liability faced by trustees.

If the committee is structured as purely advisory without responsibility for making final decisions, members should not face fiduciary liability. The final decision about distributions lies with the trustee. This is a crucial point. The DC is a resource for the trustee to fulfill the distributive function wisely and well. The ability truly to bring the distributive function to life, without incurring fiduciary liability, makes the DC a very attractive place for a family's most trusted leaders, friends, or counselors.

The DC could start out as a committee of one; it may include several members. It could even be composed of officers from a company that the trustee hires because they possess the requisite psychological and trustscape knowledge described above.

Drafting Points

We want to share some guidance to potential drafters based on what we have seen work well in our practice. The following comments are not meant to constitute legal advice, nor should they take the place of competent counsel's recommendations to you based on knowledge of your family's particular circumstances.

Ideally, the formation of the DC is authorized within the trust document. That way, there will be no question that the trustee can share information with the DC and compensate members of the DC for their work.

Another reason for including the DC in the document is to connect the work of the DC with language that specifies the overall intent of the trust. For example, we recommend that trust creators begin their trusts with such language as, "This trust is a gift of love. It exists to enhance the lives of the beneficiaries." This language provides the trustee and DC the authority to be generous and venturesome in making distributions to enhance beneficiaries' lives (rather than to subsidize them with "safe" annuities).

Finally, including the DC in the trust document clarifies that the DC exists for the life of the trust. As long as the trust has a distributive function, the trustee should have access to a DC.

If an existing trust does not include the DC role, it may be possible to use a settlement, reformation, decanting, or even a broadly empowered trust protector to add a DC to the trust instrument. (For more on making changes to existing trusts, see Chapter 17.) It is also possible that a trustee may want to convene a DC on his or her own initiative. Again, the trustee is not ceding to the DC any of his or her fiduciary responsibility.

The trustee may not have occasion to evaluate discretionary distribution requests for many years, so the names of the members of the DC do not have to be specified in the trust. As the time for making distributions approaches, the trust document may give the trust creator, the trustee, or an independent third party the authority to appoint members to the DC. We suggest that this be done in consultation with the primary beneficiary or beneficiaries, as the DC works for the trustee, but its goal is to get to know the beneficiaries.

Once the DC is up and running, it is customary for each member to nominate his or her successor, again, in consultation with the trustee and the primary beneficiary or beneficiaries. For the coherence of the DC, authority to approve appointment of a nominee rests with the existing members. If the existing members of the DC fail to approve a nominated successor, then the authority to appoint a successor reverts to the trustee in consultation with the primary beneficiary, and the trustee's appointment thereafter is final.

The trustee is given the power to remove a member of the DC at the request of a primary beneficiary, or at the request of the other members of the DC.

It may take time for members of the DC to get to know a beneficiary; we find that 5-year terms provide continuity and stability. At the same time, changes in the lives of the Committee members and in the beneficiary's own life make it wise to limit the terms of each member to two (a total of 10 years). It is also wise to require members to age out at 70. It is not unusual for DCs to include different members at different stages of the beneficiary's life. The DC should evolve alongside the beneficiary's own evolution and development.

We recommend that the DC receive a formal review at least every three years from a panel made up of the trustee, the trust protector (if there is one), and the primary beneficiaries. This review can be part of an overall review by the protector of the health of the trustee-beneficiary relationship or its own, stand-alone activity. Such a review is a helpful foundation for the trust protector's judicial/mediative function in the system.

One can imagine a scenario in which a trustee consistently ignores or rejects the advice of a DC. Since the DC is strictly advisory, it would not have the power to overrule the trustee. This is where, in our model (described in Chapters 19–21), the judicial function of the trust protector becomes important. If the trustee is ignoring the recommendations that the DC has developed through its conversations with the primary beneficiaries, then it is likely that a breakdown has also occurred between the trustee and the beneficiaries. This would be the time for the beneficiaries to "turn on" the trust protector to investigate the situation and, if necessary, remove the trustee.

In our model, the trust protector will also seek to get to know the beneficiary, understand his or her distribution requests, and talk such requests over with the trustee. However, while the qualities desired in a DC are very similar to the qualities that you might look for in a trust protector in the model that we advocate, the two roles should not be combined. The trust protector will have a single, clearly defined judiciary role.

If it turns out that a DC simply cannot be organized, then it may make sense for similar functions to the DC's to rest in an Office of the Beneficiary (as described in Chapters 19–21). The OTB can be staffed with the same people or similar ones as would staff a DC. The beneficiary can also ask the trustee to work with the OTB on all issues related to discretionary distributions.

Appendix 4

Private Trust Companies

For some families, the desire to control their wealth management and to ensure that their wealth plays a positive role in the family's life extends beyond the use of individual trusts. For such families, a private trust company (PTC) might be an appropriate tool. This appendix will share an outline of what a PTC is, its major elements and functions, and some possible uses of PTCs. As with trusts themselves, a PTC is a complicated structure whose form and function will depend very much on its jurisdiction and the specifics of its operating agreement. Please consult legal counsel with expertise in PTCs for more on how to adapt such a tool to your family's circumstances.

Definitions

As the name implies, a PTC is a company rather than a trust. Its purpose is to serve as trustee for a family's trusts, thereby replacing or supplementing individual trustees or other institutional trust-ees. The "private" in its name implies that the company exists for the sake of trusteeing a specific family's trusts and that it is (most likely) owned by that same family. It is thus distinguished from other commercial trust companies that serve many families and that are most typically owned by a variety of stakeholders or shareholders.

Like any other business, a PTC must register for operations in a state that allows PTCs. Several states have made laws that govern the process of applying for a charter to create a PTC in those states. The details of the process depend on the state. It usually involves ensuring that the PTC will have at least one manager who is a resident of the state. It generally also requires that the approved PTC hold surety of several million dollars to protect clients and other stakeholders in the case of a significant loss or damage. PTCs face additional regulations, heavy or light, depending on the state in which they are created, including regulations around reporting on their finances and business activities to the appropriate state offices. A PTC may also have federal securities or banking reporting requirements, depending on its operations.

In short, though private and focused on the well-being of a single family, a PTC is a business operating within the highly complicated and regulated world of finance. It needs to be managed as a business with appropriate counsel and oversight if it is to achieve its desired objectives.

PTCs versus Individual Trustees

Families most often decide to set up a PTC for the sake of control: a PTC allows a family to replace individual trustees with an institutional trustee—the PTC—that they founded, own, and control. The PTC becomes the family's "go-to" trustee, and the family's trusts become the PTC's "trust clients."

The specific reasons families may choose a PTC over individual trustees are various:

1. It is extremely difficult to find individual trustees who are deeply trusted and deeply knowledgeable about a family and its values and ethos.
2. Once found, individual trustees have limited life spans—they can become diminished or otherwise incapacitated, and they die.
3. When a trustee is removed or dies, the search for a new trustee begins anew. Then the new trustee must be educated about the trusts and the family, which takes time and often dilutes the strength of the family connection enjoyed with the previous trustee.
4. Most families who choose to use a PTC have many, many trusts to trustee. A PTC can take advantage of the economies of scale in overseeing dozens or even hundreds of trusts in a way that no individual can, no matter how organized.
5. Individual trustees are also exposed to litigation by unhappy beneficiaries. Many individuals—particularly those most qualified by long experience and business success—are reluctant to serve as trustees for just this reason.
6. Individual trustees can be strongly swayed by the pleas of a beneficiary, even a beneficiary who is misdirected about his or her own good.

In contrast, PTCs don't die or become disabled. A family with a PTC does need to find trusted individuals to serve as managers of the PTC. But when one manager leaves and a new manager is introduced, the PTC itself retains the "institutional memory" that ensures a smooth transition. PTCs' limited liability status shields their owners and their managers from the liability of lawsuits alleging breach of fiduciary duty from beneficiaries (except in cases of fraud or willful negligence). Since PTCs are governed by a board of managers independent of the family, they are less likely to be swayed by the personal agendas of misdirected and disconnected beneficiaries.

The legal status of a PTC and its managers underscores this last point. Individual trustees are subject to a whole range of emotional responses that can cloud their judgment. Its separate structural, legal existence allows the PTC, as an entity, to function without emotion. Further, individual trustees have a fiduciary duty to the beneficiaries of the trusts they trustee: this duty is the source of the individual trustees' liability and hence the fear they may have about lawsuits from unhappy beneficiaries. In contrast, while a PTC (as trustee) has a fiduciary duty to the beneficiaries of the trusts of which it is the trustee, the individuals who serve as managers of a PTC do not have such a duty. Their fiduciary duty is to the PTC itself. As such, the managers of a PTC have little or no liability with respect to beneficiaries and, hence, are less likely to act out of fear of such liability. True, angry beneficiaries may sue the PTC itself. But it likely has little in the way of assets that would be subject to adjudication in such a suit.

As mentioned, a PTC is an institutional trustee. But that does not mean that it has to serve all the functions of trustee alone. A PTC may choose to partner with a (commercial) institutional trustee that is directed to handle the administrative functions of trustee. The PTC then can focus on investment management and the distributive function. This kind of partnership can nicely allow each institutional co-trustee to do the work it does best.

Governance

A PTC is governed by a board of managers that can include family members as well as individuals independent of the family (that is, who are not close relatives or otherwise subject to control by the family). The managers oversee all the various fiduciary functions of the PTC, including the acceptance, management, or termination of the PTC's trust "clients." The independent managers (not the family managers, if any) also have authority and responsibility with respect to the governance of the PTC, the governance of entities owned by the PTC's trust clients, and, very importantly, discretionary distributions from trust clients. The ability to select the board of managers is one of the main reasons that a family may choose a PTC over other institutional trustees. In particular, this freedom allows the family to appoint managers who have a diversity of specialized skills and knowledge, including expertise in the qualitative aspects of trust relationships.

One of the main questions any beneficiary is likely to ask is, "Who decides whether or not I get a distribution?" Except in the case of fully mandatory distributions, the answer in the case of a PTC would be the independent managers of the PTC.

As a company, a PTC itself has an owner. In the case of most PTCs, that owner is a trust whose sole purpose is to own the PTC. The trustee of this "owner trust" would, as the owner of its PTC, have the power to appoint and remove the PTC's managers. As a result, that trustee holds a very important position in the PTC-family system. In addition, the trustee of the "owner trust" usually has the power to appoint his or her successor, thereby ensuring the transfer of control and governance from one generation to the next.

Because of this clear corporate ownership structure, a PTC offers families the benefit of transparency in their governance. As families grow and their businesses or trusts become more complicated, it is often hard to know who decides what and how. A PTC does not eliminate the possibility of disagreements that might obstruct decisions. But if structured carefully, it would help ensure that all interested parties—beneficiaries, officers of the PTC, managers of the PTC, and the trustee of the "owner trust"—understand the process for decision making and know who the decision makers are.

Best Practices

Again, as a business, a PTC needs to be run in a business-like fashion, including with proper accounting and financial safeguards and with close attention to tax and investment laws, rules, and regulations. The managers of the PTC need to understand the traditional duties of a trustee and be able to exercise independent discretion (if they are overseeing distributions). We are not going to dwell on these matters, which are common to every financial business, but rather we hope to share some best practices that we have seen families use effectively with PTCs in particular, to ensure that they play a positive role in families' lives over generations.

First, because a PTC has many stakeholders, one best practice is to hold an annual or biennial meeting of the beneficiaries of the PTC's trust clients, managers of the PTC, and trustee(s) of the "owner trust." The purpose of this meeting would be for the managers and owners to share some understanding of their work in the prior year and to ask the beneficiaries and other family members for their questions, concerns, and thoughts on how the PTC could be made even more effective. In turn, the meeting would also be an occasion for the beneficiaries and other family members to affirm the managers' work in the prior year. Because of its formal structure, it is easy for the managers of the PTC and the beneficiaries of the client trusts to become disengaged from each other. This disengagement can breed suspicion in beneficiaries and can sap the energy of the managers. Holding this type of annual or biennial meeting can keep beneficiaries informed and managers energized.

A second helpful practice is to capture the family's values and ethos in ways that the independent managers of the PTC can use this information when making important decisions, including decisions about discretionary distributions. Often, the family's own history can be a rich resource from which to draw an understanding of its values and ethos. When managers of the PTC understand that history, they can apply those values in their decisions, along with their own good judgment and experience. In the appendix, we describe a process by which a family can capture its history and philosophy in just such a form, in a tool we call a Family Trust Review (which we describe at more length in Appendix 5). Whatever form works best—a Family Trust Review, a letter of intentions or wishes from the creator of the wealth, an "ethical will" or video testament—it is important to make sure that family's values and ethos find their way into the governance and management structure of the PTC.

Third, it is crucial not to ignore the role of the owner trust's trustee, which governs all the rest of the PTC. Given the rights and responsibilities of the trustee of the trust that will own the PTC, that individual (or group of individuals) would likely serve as the family leader in each generation. As a best practice, families with a PTC should make sure that the owner trustee is steeped in the ethos and values of the family and should understand its history. In some families, as time goes on, few if any family members serve as managers of the PTC; instead, family members take responsibility at the level of the owner trust.

Fourth, and building upon the last point, even the most soundly constructed PTC will not function well if a great majority of family members feel disconnected from its operations and decisions. That is why the annual or biennial meeting is the first best practice we described. To build on that practice, it is also important to make sure that family members are not only knowledgeable but also engaged. A key step in promoting engagement is to invite family members into the process of articulating the mission or vision of the PTC. This is not something that needs to happen every year or even every few years. But every generation, at least, should have the sense that it has added its voice to the PTC's mission or vision. Like the proverbial reed, which can bend with the wind while a sturdy oak snaps in half, a PTC should be flexible enough to adapt to the new views and attitudes of each generation rather than rigidly suppressing new ideas until litigation arises.

Fifth, and in the same spirit as the fourth best practice, a wisely managed PTC will serve as the locus for family education generally, as it can serve to design and promote a family educational program. A family wealth educational program can cover many areas, including:

- The purposes, governance, and management of the PTC.
- The differences between the family and the PTC, including the expectations for the performance and compensation of managers, including family members who are managers.

Sixth and finally, the creation of a PTC could allow for the introduction of a powerful education agent into the system, namely, the Office of the Beneficiary. We have described the Office of the Beneficiary—along with the Distribution Committee, which can very effectively serve a PTC's board of managers—in detail in Part Four of this book, so we will not repeat that description here. We mention this Office and the Distribution Committee because they fit particularly effectively within the structure of a PTC. It is important to remember that each beneficiary must choose to "activate" (and pay for) his or her OTB. But the PTC can keep the plans and resources ready should a specific beneficiary make that choice.

As an aside, with a PTC in place it may seem unnecessary to have a trust protector serving in the judicial role that we described in Chapter 21. After all, the PTC is controlled by the family, and presumably central to its mission is the long-term cultivation of family strength. However, since "the family" and so the PTC do not necessarily represent each and every beneficiary's individual point of view, we do believe that it remains important to have a wise and trusted trust protector available to adjudicate disputes between a beneficiary and the PTC. Beneficiaries' voices must be heard if they are to flourish, and the "judicial" trust protector is the ultimate protection of those voices.

´ To summarize, for some families—usually with significant business ventures and a desire to exert control over truly multi-generational wealth—a PTC can serve as a highly effective tool. It is, in the end, only a tool. The time that family members and independent managers spend on developing their own under-standing and ability to work together will determine whether that tool serves a positive and fulfilling function.

Appendix 5

Family Trust Review

Purpose

Wise Counsel Research Associates' Family Trust Review guides family leaders in designing or redesigning complex trust systems in order to integrate family values and history and to create a structure that will support the family's flourishing for decades to come. It is particularly applicable for families with multigenerational trusts, family offices, and/or a private trust company (PTC).

Content

The content of a Family Trust Review will vary by family, but it generally includes the following components:

- Summary of the family history, including short bios of family leaders, past and present.

- History of the family enterprise and philanthropy.
- Summary of prominent family values.
- Description of the existing system of trusts, including their architecture, interactions, and costs.
- Recommendations for trust system design and for family education.

Process

To create a Family Trust Review, our consultants:

- Interview family leaders.
- Study published and unpublished accounts of the history of the family and the family enterprise.
- Review existing structures and documents.

Our recommendations are based on our several decades of experience working with families with significant wealth as well as our ongoing research into the best practices of family enterprises that have succeeded over multiple generations. We also draw recommendations from our books, including *Family Wealth, Cycle of the Gift*, and *Voice of the Rising Generation*—all published by Bloomberg Press—and *TrustWorthy*, published by Trustscape LLC.

Why Commission a Family Trust Review?

A Family Trust Review helps enterprising families meet the major challenges that threaten their long-term success.

Over 70 percent of families fail to retain control over their wealth when they go through a generational transition. Why?

- 15 percent due to poor tax planning or lackluster investment performance.

- 25 percent due to inadequate education of heirs.
- 60 percent due to poor family communication and conflict.

Conversely, the 30 percent of families that do succeed in maintaining family control over the wealth:

- Commit to managing wealth as a family enterprise.
- Integrate the wishes of individual family members into a family mission-statement to guide decision making.
- Educate family members in the skills important to maintaining family unity.[1]

These findings are corroborated by recent research that we have conducted at Wise Counsel Research, focused on families that have succeeded in preserving large-scale family enterprises through at least two generational transitions. The following practices contribute to these families' success:

- Identifying a shared sense of purpose and values.
- Building family community across generations.
- Professionally managing business and financial activities.
- Continually adapting to new circumstancing and building resilience.
- Freely choosing to remain partners in business.
- Actively developing family members' skills and knowledge.
- Sharing a commitment to give back and create a family legacy.

By combining family history and values with a thoughtful design of a family's trust system, the Family Trust Review marries culture with structure.

Opportunities for Commissioning a Family Trust Review

There are several reasons that can prompt the commissioning of a Family Trust Review:

- To review existing trust structures as part of a generational transition.
- To educate trustees, beneficiaries, and managers of PTCs or family offices.
- To prepare for a transition in family or trust leadership.
- To prepare for an eventual trust termination or significant distribution of principal.
- To guide trust decanting or reformation or to redesign the architecture of complex and costly trust systems.
- To inform the creation of new trusts or a PTC.

Note

1. These findings are adapted from Roy Williams and Vic Preisser, *Preparing Heirs* (San Francisco, CA: Robert Reed, 2003).

Appendix 6

Reflections on the Often Unexpected Consequences of the Creation of a Perpetual Trust[1]

By James E. Hughes Jr., Esq.

During the past 30 years, many attorneys and financial planners in the United States have recommended that their clients create perpetual trusts. These trusts are frequently referred to as dynasty trusts. While there are a number of individual and family reasons that might propel an individual to create such a trust, in large measure the motivating factor has been to avoid the federal generation-skipping tax on the assets of trusts for later family generations. Spurred by this method of tax avoidance, a cottage industry in perpetual trusts has come into being. It has now reached sufficient scale that a number of states interested in competing for this trust business have eliminated their rules against perpetuities[2] to permit the creation of perpetual trusts within their boundaries. In doing so they joined a number of states that had never adopted this "rule." These new statutes are overturning some 300-plus years of statutes and common law precedents in England and America founded on the principle that trusts for individuals, as opposed to charities, should not be permitted to last indefinitely. It is my observation that this emphasis on tax saving as the motive for the creation of perpetual trusts and the resulting changes in statutory and precedential law to meet this motive have frequently obscured critical thinking by planners and trust founders on how the lives of the beneficiaries living within such trusts will be affected by their existence and of how society as a whole may view the existence of such trusts. In this reflection, I will endeavor to bring to light these issues so that planners and founders may consider them in determining how the perpetual trusts they are intending to create will be of the greatest benefit to the individuals for whom the trusts are being created.

Before moving to the specific issues of how a perpetual trust affects the life of its beneficiaries, I believe a review of the history of perpetual trusts will be helpful. The trust, as we know it, evolved in England and on the European continent, particularly in France, out of the Roman idea of "use." This is the legal concept that provides that a person may have the use of a thing, or *res,* for a period of time without also having the underlying ownership of that thing. This idea took root in the English and French common laws as the trust, and by the time of the Crusades it was well established in land titles. At this time the law made no distinction regarding the terms of trusts, thus permitting trusts to last indefinitely or, if you will, perpetually. Rather quickly, the nobility of England and France saw that by placing their lands in perpetual trusts they could, theoretically, perpetuate their class position indefinitely. It, therefore, became common that much of England's and France's land found its way into perpetual trusts.[3]

Unfortunately for the economies of the countries where this system developed there were two unintended consequences. First, the land in trust could often not be alienated even though the noble family had need of money or in some cases had disappeared. Second, such lands were often poorly administered, as they had no owner who cared about their improvement since he or she would never own them outright. Many beneficiaries of the life interests in the trusts sought to receive the maximum annual return possible without regard to such a policy's long-term effect on the land's productivity. The result of these unintended consequences was that a portion of England's and France's wealth was seen by its rising commercial classes to be wasted. Equally, those who had money and the creativity of the entrepreneur were frustrated as they could not buy and improve this land, thus further exacerbating the perceived negative affect of the perpetual trust on the economy. In addition, the suspension of vesting of property, as a result of perpetual trusts, often led to certain members or even whole generations of noble families becoming "trust funders" and falling into the same lassitude or remittance addiction as we often see today in some of the third- and fourth-generation members of the great families of nineteenth-century Industrial America. Often then, as now, the cause of this lassitude resulted from the fact that no member of that "noble" family ever owned or would own the capital locked up in the trust from which they received their monthly stipends, nor would any family member ever be required to learn to manage these assets. In fact, work in commerce of any kind was seen as beneath the dignity of such personages. The result of these perpetual trusts in England was that by the end of the seventeenth century, the perpetual trust came to be seen by lawyers, merchants, and economists as a substantial drag on commerce (since so much land could not be purchased or sold) and as an abuse of the original idea of trust, that, a period of suspension of ownership while another "used" something could be beneficial to commerce. The result of these concerns was the adoption in England, in the late 1600s, of the rule against perpetuities. At the time this "rule," first by case law and then by statute, was adopted, lawyers, judges, economists, and parliamentarians, therefore, saw it as a great reform.

The history of the perpetual trust in France is also instructional. France had, historically, a well-understood perpetual trust provision. However, until its revolution in 1789, France made no such reform as the English made with their rule against perpetuities. In France the absence of such a reform and the resulting restriction on the growth of France's economy, caused by the inability to purchase and sell land, slowed the country's development as a modern economy. The perceived abuse of the economy, through the use of the perpetual trust by the nobility, was seen by Napoleon and the jurists who advised him to be so serious that in 1805 in the *Code Napoleon* he eliminated the trust altogether in France. Today, a number of French lawyers are attempting to reintroduce the trust through a legal entity called the "fiducie," as they feel the lack of this vehicle has held back their clients' ability to properly plan their estates. However, none of the advocates of the "fiducie" are suggesting that such an entity be perpetual.

So what can we say historically about perpetual trusts? We can say that at least at one time in the evolution of the law of trusts, the perpetual trust existed, had a history that we can study, and that that history shows that such trusts were perceived by their respective societies to have had a significant negative impact on the marketplace and to have perpetuated a nonproductive class of people. As to the first of society's objections to the perpetual trust, there is no doubt about such trusts' historically negative impact on land sales and acquisitions.[4] As to the second, the histories of France and Russia have not been kind to a class of people who society perceives as never needing to earn their own livings, and, particularly unkind to those who enjoy such a status just because an ancestor who they often never even know, but from whom they happen to have luckily descended, created a perpetual trust for his or her descendants.

As I move toward a discussion of the supposedly new idea of a perpetual trust, I am reminded of the extremely wise admonition by George Santayana that "those who cannot remember the past are condemned to repeat it." I wonder how many of the multitude of financial planners who glibly advertise "dynasty" trusts as a product and rush them off the shelf to solve a tax problem have studied and know the history of the "first" chapter in the life of the perpetual trust as discussed above? I wonder how many of them understand that many previous societies have found the creation of a perpetual leisure class unacceptable? It is not my purpose in this article to offer an opinion on these questions but rather to raise them so that we, as planners, can meet this wise man's admonition about "remembering the past" and form a thoughtful view about them. If we do so, I believe that we can best advise our clients on the possible outcomes of the plans they are creating.

Turning now to the issues affecting the life of a beneficiary of a perpetual trust, let's first look at three issues that would not normally be first thoughts in the minds of tax planners but are often the first thoughts of caring professionals concerned about the long-term effects of their actions on the lives of their clients; on the families of which they are a part; and on the systems within which they live and operate: Heisenberg's law of unintended or unexpected consequences; the interest of society in the outcomes of the individual decisions of its members and society's ability to impact these decisions; and the Second Law of Thermodynamics, the law of entropy. Werner Heisenberg suggested that modern physics informs us that there are often unintended or unexpected consequences of acts the universe performs. Increasingly, modern economists, social scientists, and psychologists are seeing this same reality in their fields and applying Heisenberg's principle to them. The ancient Greeks understood this reality long before Heisenberg and his modern disciples and expressed it when they were preparing young men and women to enter the service professions by admonishing them to "do no harm." The ancient Greeks recognized that rushing to do good before understanding the whole system and all the issues within it that relate to the problem attempting to be solved often led to doing more harm than good. I would synthesize Heisenberg and the Greeks, then, by suggesting that, as there are often unintended or unexpected consequences of what we do and some of what we do may do harm, as we begin any planning project, we begin with the rule "first be sure to do no harm before you attempt to do good." This rule is particularly applicable to the creation of a perpetual trust. Why? Because the planner is mortal and the trust he or she is creating is theoretically immortal. Certainly, in such a case, many questions regarding the natures and experiences of the descendants of the trust's founder, and the environment in which they and the trust will exist will not only not be known or discernable by the founder but will also not be known by or discernable by the planner. The planner in assisting the founder in creating such a trust must recognize that he or she will be significantly impacting the lives of each of the trustee's beneficiaries, as each beneficiary in turn integrates the trust's existence into his or her own. I would suggest that it ought to be a humbling experience for trust planners and trust founders to imagine what life might be like for these beneficiaries even just two or three generations from those alive today, much less the seventh, eighth, and ninth and those generations thereafter. Perhaps, the admonition of the Iroquois elders to each other as they began important tribal work that "it should be our hope that the members of the tribe seven generations from now will honor us for the care and thoughtfulness we exercise in our decision making today" would be helpful to planners and founders of perpetual trusts as they begin their work. Rightly, the creation of a perpetual trust affecting so many generations of a family ought to be done and entered into with great humility and plenty of patience. The thought "hasten slowly" comes to mind.

Moving to planning for a perpetual trust's creation, I strongly suggest that every planner carefully consider all the possible impacts the trust may have on the lives of its beneficiaries, particularly its unintended consequences, and bring those thoughts to the attention of the trust's potential founder. By so alerting the trust's founder the planner will be trying to eliminate to the greatest extent possible the negative impact the trust might have on these beneficiaries and meet his/her highest responsibility to the founder and the beneficiaries to "do no harm." Strangely, in the rush to get the tax work done and to "get the papers out," all too often, I observe that the trust's impact on the lives of its beneficiaries is never discussed. This failure to take the time to consider these issues may be, from the founder's standpoint, and his or her intention to benefit the beneficiaries, by enhancing their lives, the greatest unintended mistake. Why? Because it may lead to the creation of a trust which diminishes the lives of its beneficiaries. Should such a result occur, the founder would have been deprived by the trust's planner of the advice he or she most needed in attempting to accomplish his or her enhancement goals.

We, as planners, owe a duty to our clients to bring all the issues that may impact a client's decisions to that client so that he or she may make the most informed decision. It is my hope that when one of our clients is thinking of creating a perpetual trust that it will be such issues:

1. as its possible negative impact on its beneficiaries by causing them to become "remittance addicted," and
2. by its depriving them of a chance to dream and the freedom to bring their dreams to life,

that will be the issues we will chose to discuss most deeply with him or her. Why? Because they are the issues where the greatest risk of unintended negative consequences lie to the lives of the beneficiaries and to the enhancement goals of the trusts' founder.

Turning to the second of my questions: society's interest in the decisions its individual members make. As I explained earlier, English, French, and Russian societies at earlier periods of history found the perpetual trust and the perpetual leisure or non–working class it created unacceptable. In America, that same anxiety about the existence of such a class led to the adoption, in the colonies, first by inheritance of the English common law and then by individual state statutes, of rules against perpetuities. These statutes expressed society's view that the suspension of the ownership of property perpetually was an unacceptable hindrance to the economy and to the movement of wealth within society as a whole. The "rule" may also express a concern in the society as a whole about a perpetually landed class that did not need to work. Again, as above, I offer no opinion on the correctness of any earlier societies' views on these subjects. I simply wish to point out to planners that this history exists, and in the case of France and arguably Russia, helped lead to revolutions. I believe it is our duty as planners to advise our clients of these histories so that they may consider all points of view before acting to create an entity that, at other times in history, certain societies have seen as unacceptable. I believe it is also important to consider that no society known to history has ever accepted within its midst a perpetually leisured or non–working class. I must say, as a historian and amateur sociologist, I cringe when I see those masterful statistical analyses created by trust planners projecting the enormous buildups of wealth within these perpetual trust entities, all designed to encourage potential trust founders to get on with buying such a product from the planner. I wonder whether the planner is currying favor with the founder's ego by suggesting the creation of such a monument to the founder all the while disguising this fact by suggesting how happy the beneficiaries will be?[5] In any event, the history of the evolution of modern human societies and their children, the cultures and civilizations formed within them, shows that society has never permitted such "monuments" to last very long, all as reflected in the history of the rise and fall of families and dynasties and in poetry; remember "Ozymandias"? I suggest that society, like biology, seeks creation and change to meet new circumstances and to allow new forms of community to arise, as Heraclitus said, "Everything is in flux." I would suggest that society dislikes the profound order found in monuments. Given this history, I would suggest that society's concerns have to be taken into account in guiding founders on the long-term likelihood that their planners projected monumental financial results will turn out to be true. Finally, I caution many readers of this piece who are now just beginning to imagine life without federal estate taxation and federal generation-skipping taxation to consider how likely it is that American society will bring both of these taxes back if it perceives that they are needed as a way to avoid a perpetual leisure or non–working class. Coming again to the law of unintended consequences, are we, as planners, re-creating the environment within American society for the reenactment of the federal estate tax and generation-skipping tax sometime in the future by the creation of perpetual trusts?

Finally, the third issue, the Second Law of Thermodynamics, the law of entropy. This law of physics reminds us that everything that is material will over time be worn away by entropy. Physics teaches that energy forms materiality, and materiality through the action of entropy dematerializes back to energy. I am not a physicist, and I apologize to the readers who are for this paraphrase of this deeply complicated concept; however, I hope they will accept it as sufficient for other nonphysicists to appreciate what entropy is and how entropy works. What does the law of entropy have to do with perpetual trusts? I suggest everything since it suggests that anything manmade that we believe is perpetual is an illusion, a mirage, or whatever other term for false vision you may prefer. This law of physics teaches us that nothing is perpetual except perhaps the never-ending process of energy in flux, order to chaos to order to chaos indefinitely. While it may be heartening to trust founders to think they are perpetually endowing the enhancement of the lives of their descendants, I strongly suggest that they be disabused of such an idea by a quick dose of the antitoxin to these dreams, the law of entropy. Planners who pander to the hubris of their clients by suggesting the creation of a perpetual trust as a monument that will endure forever are pandering to their clients' worst instincts. Rather, bringing the law of entropy into the conversation brings both planner and founder back to humility and the awareness that in their work together toward the creation of a legal entity that will impact others' lives, and particularly a perpetual trust with its intended extended period of life, they must be sure *they will do no harm before they try to do good*.

I cannot urge more strongly that planners bring before and discuss with potential founders of perpetual trusts these three important realities:

1. There will be unintended consequences of this perpetual trust, so have we considered as many possible outcomes of the creation of this trust as we can imagine, with our greatest focus being on those that may decrease rather than those that increase the pursuits of individual happiness of the beneficiaries of the trust? Have we used the seventh-generation wisdom of the Iroquois? Have we hastened slowly? Have we asked: "What harm will we do before we try to do good"?
2. Society will have a view about and an impact on this perpetual trust, so: Have we considered what society's view and impact might be, and have we considered it not just from the viewpoint that society is adverse to what we may first perceive as our goal of having a trust last perpetually but that perhaps society may have a valid point of view that

might cause us to modify how we go forward? Have we at least considered that society as a system will in some way impact and even constrain our goals of having a trust last perpetually?

3. The law of entropy is alive and well and informs us that nothing material is forever so: Have we brought this law of physics into our consciousness as we plan and have we imagined how it will impact the life and operation of the perpetual trust?

Arguably, most of the impacts of the three core questions set out above appear to be external forces bearing on the founder's decisions regarding the perpetual trust. I would argue, however, that the most significant risk to the success of a perpetual trust (which success I define as a trust that, over a long period of time, actually enhances the lives of its beneficiaries) is internal. It is the risk that because of a lack of internal governance of the relationship between the beneficiaries and the trustees, the trust will not enhance the lives of its beneficiaries but rather will diminish them. I suggest the problem lies in Walt Kelly's Pogo's astute observation about much of the dysfunction in human behavior, which is that "he went searching for the enemy and found it was us"; in other words, the trust's planners, the trust's founders, and its beneficiaries themselves are the cause of the trust's failure to prove enhancing to its beneficiaries. In my practice, it is common to meet beneficiaries of trusts who tell me that the trust has been a net negative in their lives. In an earlier book, *Family Wealth: Keeping It in the Family,* and in two papers, "The Trustee as Mentor," and "The Trustee as Regent within a Family Governance System," co-authored with Patricia Angus, I discussed at length the issues faced by beneficiaries of trusts. In those works, I pointed out that the relationship between a trustee and beneficiary is like an arranged marriage since neither chooses the other when the relationship is formed. Necessarily, for Western Hemisphere readers, such relationships are likely to be volatile and not ones we would choose if given a chance. Certainly, they would fail my test for any partnership, an affirmative answer to the question, "Can I be your partner?" That is, can I give myself whole-heartedly to you, my partner? I also pointed out that in these relationships it is a rare beneficiary who has any training on how to be an excellent beneficiary. It is not, therefore, surprising that most beneficiaries do not govern this relationship well. Often, in fact, the beneficiary has no real understanding of the roles and responsibilities he or she is to assume as a beneficiary and will be expected to perform in the beneficiary-trustee relationship. Almost never, in my experience, can the beneficiary understand that he or she is expected to comprehend that at the heart of this relationship is the concept that he or she should control this relationship without owning the underlying assets. Separate from the relationship difficulties, and often in my experience much more serious, is the very real possibility that the beneficiary will fall victim to becoming "remittance addicted." This is a state of life in which a human being's human and intellectual capitals are in entropy. It is the life of a beneficiary of a trust where the individual is unable to imagine, metaphorically, a life without the check from the trustee at the beginning of the month. Such persons are seen by the psychological profession as exhibiting the same dysfunctional characteristics as persons addicted to alcohol, drugs, gambling, and so on. Anyone who is addicted is by definition not free. It is hard to imagine that any founder of a perpetual trust, making a gift of love by transferring his or her ownership of financial capital into the care of a trustee for the purpose of enhancing the lives of the trust's beneficiaries, would choose to create an entity that might, and sadly often does, create exactly the opposite effect and outcome. Every trust, perpetual or with a fixed term, carries with it the risk of this outcome for its beneficiaries. Planners who are seeking to truly guide their clients will always offer this enlightened and educated view of the possible outcome of trusts to their clients. The sharing of such views is particularly important in the case of perpetual trusts. Why? Because the laws of demographic probability suggest that there will be a geometric increase in the possible beneficiaries of such trusts in each later family generation. Thus, through the normal birth rates expected within families, such trusts are more likely to spawn such remittance-addicted persons than fixed-term trusts since more people over time will be exposed to the possibility of becoming so addicted. The potential founders of perpetual trusts are entitled to be made aware of this potentiality.

Another reality of trusts of all kinds is that many beneficiaries do not: (a) feel worthy of the gift of being a beneficiary and (b) find the trust a hindrance to their development, to their sense of how free they are to make their own life choices; and (c) to their sense of self-worth. While to the average person without a trust this may seem a strange thought, it is in fact one of the realities of trust life. Many beneficiaries feel that the trust saps them of creativity and of the excitement of creating something of their own. They sincerely wonder who they might be if the trust did not exist, would they be happier, and would they be more esteeming of their own unique abilities and gifts. In addition, they feel beholden to someone they often will never meet, whose history they are expected to admire, appreciate, and emulate. Why, they ask, when it is only through a "DNA" shuffle that they bear any relation to him or her. In fact, they may be embarrassed by his or her history while being locked by the trust into it. Again, as in other parts of this paper, I take no view on the rightness or wrongness of beneficiaries' views on this subject. It is rather my goal that these often expressed concerns of beneficiaries be brought to the attention of potential trust founders so they can include them in their thinking.

Yet another reality of trust life is nonmentoring as opposed to mentoring trustees. In my experience, many trusts fail their founders' hopes that they will enhance the lives of their beneficiaries because the trustees of such trusts themselves go into entropy. Often, trustees fail to change with the times and bring outdated thinking to new problems. Worse, some trustees begin to see themselves as the real owners of the trust's property, acting as if they are the founders' alter-egos rather than the beneficiary's representatives, and begin to believe they know better than the beneficiaries how the beneficiaries should live their lives. They become unchosen parents and, worse, autocrats when in reality their role is to serve the growth and development of the beneficiaries as human beings and as intellectual creatures. Too often, and especially in the later years of a long-lived trust when the founder is long dead and the trustees never knew him or her, the trustees begin to identify themselves and their stations in life by the trust's assets and start doing and acting accordingly, forgetting that they are the servants of the beneficiaries and of future generations of beneficiaries to come.

We turn now to special issues of trust governance posed by perpetual trusts. Thoughtful planners who suggest the formation of perpetual trusts and the founders who create them will realize that there is a heightened possibility of failed trust governance when the relationship between the beneficiaries and the trustee will last for a very extended period of time. All trust governance is at risk of failure, on the beneficiary side by the beneficiary becoming remittance addicted, and on the trustee side by the trustees falling into entropy and self-dealing. Unfortunately, when a perpetual period is chosen for a trust, these risks are heightened, since there is simply more time for the law of entropy to work its will in the beneficiaries' and trustees' negative experiences of the trust and of their relationship with each other. Happily, today enlightened planners have an armentarium of planning antidotes to protect beneficiaries and trustees against failed trust governance. I believe one in particular is relevant here. I believe the most important antidote to failed trusts' governance is selecting mentoring trustees who will actively work with the beneficiaries to achieve the founders' goals of enhancing the beneficiaries lives through the growth of their individual human and intellectual capitals. Unfortunately, nothing will protect beneficiaries from themselves if the law of entropy acting through the trust's negative forces have made them dependent persons, a process that nonmentoring trustees will always accelerate. Mentoring trustees working to create excellent relationships with their beneficiaries and beneficiaries working to become excellent beneficiaries in managing their relationships with their trustees have real possibilities of success. It is in the good management of these relationships that the trust's purpose to enhance the lives of its beneficiaries' has a reasonable prospect of success. As the trustees and beneficiaries begin this process of self-government, what are some of the outcomes for the beneficiaries they might consider so that the trust, whether perpetual or fixed term, will provide the greatest enhancement for its beneficiaries' lives. I would suggest that beneficiaries and trustees begin by recognizing that philosophy teaches that for each beneficiary, the goals

1. of becoming fully self-aware and achieving personal freedom so as to be able to live an independent life;
2. of achieving the fulfillment of his or her life's dreams through knowing and fulfilling his or her life's calling; and
3. of being able to take full responsibility for his or her actions

are goals of high value and purpose. I would suggest that every effort by the trustees and the beneficiaries should be toward the end of achieving these results for the beneficiaries if the trust is to meet the founder's original goal that the trust enhance the life of each of its beneficiaries. I worry that in a perpetual trust the beneficiaries may say why should I worry about becoming an excellent beneficiary and about trust governance, and do all the hard work of making this relationship work, if neither I nor my children nor my descendants, in any generation, will ever own the assets? Why should I try to learn to be a good steward? Why should I work? Be an apprentice? Find my calling? When I can do nothing! Who will ask the beneficiary the questions that will help him or her understand that these questions must be answered if he or she is to achieve a full share of independence and self-worth? Let's hope that founders will be alerted to these questions and realities by their planners and both provide language for their beneficiaries within their trusts that raise these questions and select trustees prepared to engage with the beneficiaries to help them find individual answers to them that will lead to their trust's enhancing the beneficiaries lives as they intended.

Perpetual trusts, as do all trusts, have the capacity to be enhancing to their beneficiaries' abilities to become self-aware and independent, to seek a calling; and to be able to take full responsibility for their actions or to do nothing and become dependent, with all the sadness such entropic lives engender. I am particularly concerned, however, about perpetual trusts because their earlier history suggests that they may have a greater risk of leading to dependence than fixed-term trusts. Whether my concerns will become reality will only be known many years from now when the second and third generations of beneficiaries of such trusts take their places. It is my hope that this article and the questions it poses will offer today's trust planners and trust founders food for thought about the impact on the lives of such beneficiaries of the trusts they work together to create. Perhaps for some of these future beneficiaries the thought and time it takes to consider these questions will lead to their trusts enhancing rather than diminishing their lives. Should such a result be achieved by some perpetual trusts it is likely that these trusts' founders will have taken Santayana's admonition about the past to heart. In addition, I feel that my work in writing this paper will in some small way have helped achieve these trusts founders' goal—the goal that through setting up such a perpetual trust they will make a gift of love to its beneficiaries, the multiple generations to come of their families; a gift that the trust's beneficiaries will perceive as the trust works to enhance their lives. Such a gift will give the beneficiaries real reason to honor and appreciate the depth of the founder's vision. Thoughtful giving begins with carefully considering whether a gift will do harm and then, after considering all its possibly harmful effects, whether it will do good.

Notes

1. Originally published in the *Chase Journal* (5:3), 2001. © Hughes & Whitaker.

2. The normal "Rule Against Perpetuities" as cited in *Scott,* 62.10: "No interest is good unless it must vest, if at all, not later than twenty-one years after some life in being at the creation of the interest. . . ."

3. While not the subject of this article, the perpetual trust was widely used by the Church to hold its land until in certain parts of England and France the Church became the largest land owner. As Europe's business environment modernized in the fifteenth and sixteenth centuries, this fact caused much dissatisfaction with the Church's secular rather than spiritual role. The resulting stultification of commerce, land being its principal medium, was seen by the Tudors in England, as highly prejudicial to England's development. As a result, many people in the economic classes warmly welcomed Henry VIII's decision as part of his "Reformation" to sequester and redistribute church property as a necessary reform needed to accelerate the development of England's economy.

4. I am aware that some readers may feel that this history is not applicable to the modern economic environment where wealth is represented far more in movable than immovable property. This article is not the place for an economic debate. I will observe only that the trustees of nearly every trust are required by the state laws that govern trusts to be "prudent in the investments they make of the trust's assets." Equally, they may make no investment that is not prudent. Creativity is defined, in the commercial area, as entrepreneuring and is all about taking risks. It is my view that creativity and the risks it entails is not included within these state law definitions of prudence and rightly so since it is someone else's assets that the trustee is administering. This reality proves unfortunate over time for trust beneficiaries. Why? Because it is a simple fact of the law of competitive risk and reward that, over time, the

trustee carrying out his responsibilities to be prudent cannot take the risks that an entrepreneur using his or her own resources can take, and so, over time, the return achieved by the trustee in competition within the marketplace with all other investors should and will be less. This logic carried out over the multiple generations assumed by a perpetual trust suggests strongly that, assuming the market is neutral, a trust's assets will fail to grow at the same rate as the market as a whole. Should this logic be true then such trusts will eventually find themselves in the same negative position commercially as those that owned but could not trade in land. At a later part of the main article, I will discuss entropy. Please apply the logic I express then to this problem of the risk and reward in the management of assets perpetually in the hands of nonentrepreneurial persons. My father always advised his business owner clients that while putting the shares of their companies into trust might appear to be the best solution to their desire for their company's perpetuation, it was his experience that trustees, who had not elected to invest in the company but, rather, had received these shares on the creation of the trust, made poor shareholders since they hadn't made the same risk-taking investment decisions that the best shareholders make. He would also add that since trustees are obliged by law to adopt a policy of diversification of risk, how well could they be expected to achieve the grantor's objectives in the face of the law's demands? Of course, "drafting" may help, but in the end judges measuring trustee performance will have the benchmarks of prudence and diversity as their measuring sticks. I suggest that these are very relevant points to consider in assessing the likely success today of perpetual trusts achieving long-term market success in the light of history's measure of them and our current knowledge of how the market works.

5. I also wonder whether these planners have studied Aristotle's view of how difficult the journey is for Western man to be happy and how much of that journey is about knowing one's self, finding useful work in calling and living out one's own dream, and how little is about inheritance of other dreams as reflected by such monuments? I suggest Confucius, Socrates, the Buddha, Gandhi, and many twentieth-century figures like Jung, Maslow, and Erickson have much also to say about this journey, each of whom in his own way comes to much the same conclusion about what processes enhance people's lives and which diminish them.

About the Authors

Hartley Goldstone JD, MBA

Following 25 years as attorney, senior trust officer, and senior staff of a multifamily office, Hartley founded Trustscape LLC in 2009 to help clients build trustscapes that harness the best in people for the greatest good. As an adviser, he offers field-tested approaches and tools to identify—and then achieve—positive possibilities in the relationship between beneficiary and trustee.

Clients include institutional and individual trustees, family offices, and beneficiaries in all stages of life.

Hartley launched the ongoing Beneficiary and Trustee Positive Story Project in 2010 to collect stories told by beneficiaries and trustees that reflect compassion and wisdom in the midst of complexity. Two years later, he co-authored *TrustWorthy*, a collection of 25 of the real-life stories. In 2013, the Positive Story

Project became the theme of his online column for the journal *Trusts & Estates*.

Hartley is a research fellow at Wise Counsel Research, a founding member of the Collaboration for Family Flourishing, dean of the Trustscape for the Purposeful Planning Institute, and a member of the International Positive Psychology Association.

He has spoken about flourishing trustscapes at conferences of the Family Office Exchange, the American College of Trust and Estate Counsel, the Institute for Private Investors, the American Bankers Association, the Purposeful Planning Institute, and many others. He is a presenter for Shaking the Tree, a not-for-profit organization with a unique theatre-based approach to enriching intergenerational conversations about wealth and purpose.

Hartley received his B.A. degree from the University of Pennsylvania, and MBA and Juris Doctor degrees from the University of Denver.

James E. Hughes Jr., Esq.

Jay, a resident of Aspen, Colorado, is a retired attorney and the author of *Family Wealth: Keeping It in the Family* and *Family—The Compact Among Generations*, co-author of *The Cycle of the Gift* and of *The Voice of The Rising Generation*, and numerous articles on family governance and wealth preservation as well as a series of Reflections, which can be found on the Articles section of his web site, www.jamesehughes.com. He was the founder of a law partnership in New York City and has spoken frequently at numerous international and domestic symposia on the avoidance of the "shirtsleeves to shirtsleeves" proverb and the growth of families' human, intellectual, social, and spiritual capital as supported by their financial capital toward their families' flourishing. He is a member of various philanthropic boards and a member of the editorial boards of various professional journals. He is a graduate of the Far Brook School, which teaches through the arts; the Pingry School; Princeton University; and the Columbia School of Law.

Dr. Keith Whitaker

Keith is founding president of Wise Counsel Research—a think-tank focused on wealth and philanthropy—and an adjunct professor of Management at Vanderbilt University Owen Graduate School of Business. He also serves as an independent trustee, trust protector, and manager of private trust companies.

Keith has many years' experience consulting with advisers to and leaders of enterprising families. He helps families plan succession, develop next generation talent, and communicate around estate planning.

Keith served as a Managing Director at Wells Fargo, where he founded the innovative Family Dynamics Practice. He has also served as a researcher at the Boston College Center on Wealth and Philanthropy; a director of a private foundation; and an adjunct assistant professor of philosophy.

With Dr. Susan Massenzio and James E. Hughes, Jr., Keith published *The Voice of the Rising Generation: Family Wealth & Wisdom* (Bloomberg, 2014) and *The Cycle of the Gift: Family Wealth & Wisdom* (Bloomberg, 2013). Keith's writings and commentary have appeared in *The Wall Street Journal, The New York Times, The Financial Times,* and *Philanthropy Magazine.* With Dr. Paul Schervish, he also published *Wealth and the Will of God* (Indiana University Press, 2010). *Family Wealth Report* named Keith the 2015 "outstanding individual contributor to wealth management thought-leadership."

Keith is a member of the Boston Estate Planning Council and a founding member of the Collaboration for Family Flourishing.

He holds a Ph.D. in Social Thought from the University of Chicago and a BA and MA in Classics and Philosophy from Boston University.

In lieu of a static bibliography here in *Family Trusts*, readers can find a regularly updated bibliography of readings related to trusts and family wealth at www.wisecounselresearch.org.

Index